BULBS

The American Horticultural Society
Illustrated Encyclopedia of Gardening

BULBS

The American Horticultural Society
Mount Vernon, Virginia

For The American Horticultural Society

President
Dr. Gilbert S. Daniels

Technical Advisory Committee
Everett Conklin
Mary Stuart Maury
Dr. John A. Wott

Bulbs Staff for The Franklin Library/Ortho Books

Editorial Director
Min S. Yee

Supervisory Editor
Lewis P. Lewis

Editor
Ken Burke

Art Directors
John Williams
Barbara Ziller

Creative Director
Michael Mendelsohn

Assistant Creative Director
Clint Anglin

Written by
James McNair

Illustrations by
Cyndie Clark-Huegel

Additional Illustrations by
Ron Hildebrand

Horticultural Consultants

John E. Bryan
Horticultural Consultant
San Francisco, California

August De Hertogh
Horticultural Science Department
North Carolina State University
Raleigh, North Carolina

Carl A. Totemeier, Jr.
Old Westbury Gardens
Old Westbury, New York

Production Director
Robert Laffler

Production Manager
Renee Guilmette

Production Assistant
Paula Green

For Ortho Books

Publisher
Robert L. Iacopi

For The Franklin Library

Publisher
Joseph Sloves

Tulips are synonomous with spring in many parts of the world, and the magnificent display shown on the front cover is a wonderful example of the joyous feeling these bulbs can give to any garden. Photograph copyright © by Derek Fell.

Flower Arranging by
Evalyn K. Bell

Special Thanks to:
Blake Gardens
Kensington, California
Gerald Clear
Cooley's Gardens
Silverton, Oregon
Ken Doty
Stan Farwig
Vic Girard
Arthur Hecht
Larry McDonald
Mr. and Mrs. Edward Mitchell
Earl Murphy
Wayne Roderick
Betty Rollins
Jack Romine
Hyacinth Smith
Sara Tuckey
Dick Turner
George Waters

Photography by
(Names of photographers in alphabetical order are followed by page numbers on which their work appears. R = right, C = center, L = left, T = top, B =bottom)

William Aplin
74LB

John Bryan
28, 29, 30L, 34BR, 37TL,CR,B, 43, 66L, 70, 107BL, 120TR, 126T, 130T

The Butchart Gardens
12–13

Clyde Childress
55L, 58TR,BL, 59

Zelma Clark
42B, 45B, 56

Josephine Coatsworth
37TR, 54, 74B, 75TR, 76R, 85T, 86, 87T, 90, 91L, 92, 93, 103T, 104(all), 105T, 113, 121(all), 122B, 127R, 132B

Karil Daniels
108B

Stan Farwig
95R, 100T, 109, 119T, 132LC, 133B

Derek Fell
95L, 96R, 101T, 102T, 106(all), 107T, 122T, 132LB, 136B

Fred Galle
102BR, 137T

Pamela Harper
115TR, 130B, 131L

International Bloembollencentrum
Hillegom, Holland
119C

Michael Landis
31, 36B, 42T, 57, 66R, 125RC

Richard Lighty
38T, 44, 85RB, 94B, 105B, 119B

Fred Lyon
73T

MALAK of Ottawa
110L

Michael McKinley
21, 35TL,BR, 58TL, 76B, 77T, 88, 89, 97, 99T, 101B, 112R, 120L,C, 136T, 137B

James McNair
35BL, 36T, 37(middle), 58BR, 85B, 100B

Paul Meyer
Morris Arboretum of the University of Pennsylvania
24, 37CL, 87BR, 98, 105C, 115B

New York Public Library Picture Collection
15

Ortho Photo Library
2, 23, 34T,BL, 35TR, 38(except T), 39, 40, 45T, 47, 53, 61, 62, 63TL,TR, 73RB,B, 74LT, 75B, 76TL, 77B, 78, 84, 87B, 111B, 123, 124(except B), 125(except RC), 131RT,RB, 133T, 134, 135T,B, 136LB, 138, 139

Picnic Productions
63B

Dr. Robert Raabe
University of California, Berkeley
83, 91R, 99B, 103B, 110R, 111T, 115CR, 126B, 127L

Regional Parks Botanic Garden
Berkeley, California
94T, 96L

Schreiner's Iris Gardens
Salem, Oregon
20, 114(all), 115TL, 116(all), 117(all), 118(all)

Jim Sikkema
67(all), 102BL, 107BR, 108T, 135C

Michael Smith
132T

Ralph Stark
11, 124B, 128TR,B

David Thomas
30R, 55R

Van Bourgondien Bros.
112L

Larry Weber
33

White Flower Farm
Litchfield, Connecticut
41

Beverly Wirth
120RB

Min Yee
65

Produced under the authorization of The American Horticultural Society by The Franklin Library and Ortho Books.

Every effort has been made at the time of publication to guarantee the accuracy of the names and addresses of information sources and suppliers and in the technical data contained. However, the subscriber should check for his own assurance and must be responsible for selection and use of suppliers and supplies, plant materials, and chemical products.

 Portions of this volume previously appeared in the Ortho Books *House Plants Indoors/Outdoors, Gardening with Color, All About Bulbs,* and *All About Perennials*.

Library of Congress Catalog Card Number 81–71123
Printed in the United States of America
12 11 10 9 8 7 6 5

A Special Message from The American Horticultural Society

Bulbs have a special place in the gardener's world. They bloom for years with little or no care. There are so many different kinds available in such a wide range of colors and sizes that there are bulbs for every purpose and place, and you can have a succession of flowers almost all year round. Some flowering bulbs make admirable houseplants. Others multiply naturally when scatter-planted in an informal landscape. Still others create a striking formal effect when grouped in mass plantings.

Bulbs gives the lie to the commonly held belief that bulbs are for spring only. And there are more than just tulips, daffodils, hyacinths, and irises to choose from. The encyclopedia section gives descriptions and cultural requirements of seventy different bulbs, with recommended cultivars and species for certain locations and climates, as well as for different seasons.

Not only do bulbs require a minimum of care, most of them are relatively disease-free, although a few precautionary procedures are given to ensure that they stay healthy. Propagating is a simple process, if it needs to be done at all. The rewards for the comparatively small effort involved in gardening with bulbs are exceptional. Even experienced gardeners will undoubtedly benefit from the sound advice and sensible information given here. Season after season, year after year, these small natural wonders liven the landscape, brighten the house, and delight the senses.

This is one of the most appealing volumes in our *Illustrated Encyclopedia of Gardening*. Once you have looked at it, read it, we think you will be unable to resist the urge to introduce bulbs into your garden. This book can add a new dimension to everyone's gardening, for years.

Gilbert S. Daniels
President

CONTENTS

A Brief History of Bulbs **10**
When bulbs were introduced in Europe in the 16th century, they revolutionized gardening. Within fifty years, people were speculating wildly in tulip bulbs, paying fantastic prices for them. Fortunes, even lives, were lost to tulipomania. But eventually tulips and other bulbs were allowed to resume a healthy development resulting in the dazzling array available today.

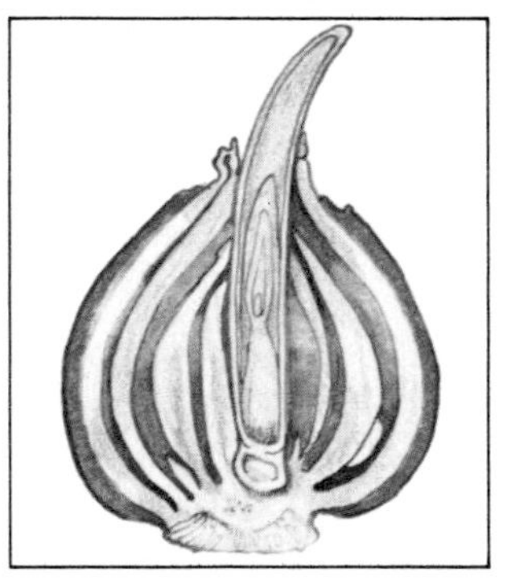

Types of Bulbs **22**
All bulbous plants store food on which they can live during periods of dormancy, but not all such plants are true bulbs. Some are large stems, others are swollen roots. This chapter discusses and illustrates the different types of bulbs, explains their growth habits, and tells how you can propagate them. An inside look at the bulb industry explains how new species are introduced.

Gardening with Bulbs 32
For the home gardener, bulbs have many possible uses and pleasures. They can provide colorful accents when mixed with other plants, they can be featured in a spectacular mass planting, they give delightful interest to a landscape when naturalized, and some are particularly suited to forcing or growing in containers. It is important to match the kind of bulb you choose to its use.

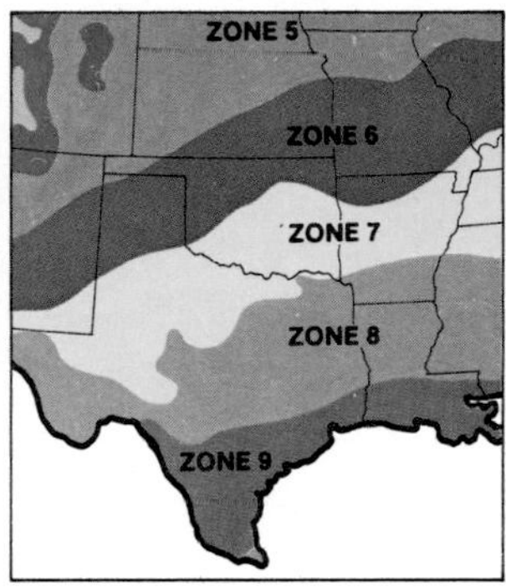

Bulbs for All Seasons 46
You can have bulbs in flower almost all year round if you plant the right bulb at the right time. This chapter suggests bulbs for each season, and provides a chart of anticipated blooming seasons that will help you plan for a succession of bulbs in flower. A section on indoor gardening explains how you can have bulbs as houseplants, either for seasonal or year-round display.

Healthy and Care-free Bulbs 64
Bulbs are easy to grow, and most are relatively pest-free. There are, however, a few protective measures you can take to keep them that way. This chapter gives tips on buying good quality bulbs; pointers on the proper site and soil for planting them; advice about good watering, fertilizing, and propagating methods; and instructions for storing bulbs when necessary.

Encyclopedia of Bulbs **82**

This chapter gives the characteristics of seventy different bulbs, with descriptions and growing requirements that will enable you to select the right bulbs for your climate, needs, and even special locations in your landscape. Certain species are named when they are noted for fragrance, color, easy or difficult care, or success as houseplants.

Mail-Order Suppliers and Plant Societies **141**

Directory of Common Names **142**

Index **143**

BULBS

The tulip's arrival in Europe from the gardens of the Ottoman Empire transformed the European concept of a garden from one of pure practicality to one of beauty.

A BRIEF HISTORY OF BULBS

The history of bulbs is a vivid one—at one time people would pay many times its weight in gold for a single tulip bulb. Bulbs still fascinate us today, but in a much more satisfying way.

Until the 16th century, gardens in Europe were generally cultivated for food, medicine, dyes, and other practical reasons. A plant might happen to be pretty, but it was rarely grown for its beauty. When trade between Western Europe and the Ottoman Empire burgeoned in the latter half of the 16th century, Europeans saw and heard of the fabulous gardens of Sultan Suleiman I and were tantalized. Recent discoveries of distant lands to the East and West with exotic and rare treasures created a thirst for more. The sultan's gardens were bursting with thousands of highly developed and cultivated tulips and hyacinths. It was as if another new world had been discovered.

Fascinated with their new find, Europeans slowly began to change their traditional approach to gardening. People came to think of gardens as places of leisure, refreshment, and visual enjoyment, rather than just as practical plots for cultivating necessary foods and medicines. It could be considered the beginning of a horticultural revolution. The tulip reached Europe around 1554, and the hyacinth appeared shortly after that. And then a flood of different bulbs arrived—some from Turkey, others from the Balkans and similar remote places.

The scholarly Charles L'Escluse (who wrote under the *nom de plume* Carolus Clusius) had much to do with the introduction of bulbs to Europe. He began as Prefect of the Royal Medicinal Garden in Prague, but was later brought to Vienna by the Emperor Maximilian II for the sole purpose of collecting bulbs from the Near East. It was to this monarch that the first tulip bulbs were sent, but the discovery was not made public until 1576, when he also introduced the Crown Imperial (*Fritillaria imperialis*). L'Escluse later moved from Vienna to the university at Leiden, Holland. There, he assumed the chair of Professor of Botany, and developed their gardens—Hortus—into one of the most famous gardens of the world. To this day, Holland remains the world center of the bulb industry.

Soon, the bulb craze overwhelmed Europe. How paradoxical that such rare and exotic beauty should flower from such homely lumps! And, as if to belie their costliness, the bulbs grew with the greatest of ease, rapidly increased themselves, shipped sound, and lasted long once out of the ground. The English herbalist John Parkinson published *A Garden of All Sorts of Pleasant Flowers*, in 1629, and by then bulbs were such a rage that he devoted over 200 pages to discussing different bulb varieties.

About 40 years later, in 1665, John Rea published the first book to set out designs for beds displaying bulbs; mostly, the bulbs were centered around designs for the walled garden. By the end of the 17th century, every great estate had a lavish display of spring bulbs. Parterres were laid out at the front of the huge houses, were formed into beds of intricate design, and filled with tulips, daffodils, and hyacinths.

In England a more naturalized design trend was introduced by William Kent. And then, thanks to Lancelot ("Capability") Brown, great estate

Tulips brighten the annual spring display at Butchart Gardens in Victoria, British Columbia.

gardens began to use fewer bulbs and more natural, wooded-parkland plants. This era lasted from the late 18th century through the mid-20th (around World War II). When estate gardens again sported plants that produced great displays of spring color, it wasn't bulbs that provided the pallette, but the exotic bedding plants produced by the improved technology of hothouse gardening.

With the development of a middle class with money and leisure time, hardy bulbs left the estates of the rich and found their way to cottage gardens and backyards. Through the late 18th and early 19th centuries, however, the wealthy favored the more exotic tender bulbs.

In 1772, Kew Gardens sent Francis Masson to South Africa to collect

plants. From there Masson and Carl Thunberg sent back many startling and previously unknown plants, including species from the genera *Amaryllis, Crinum, Agapanthus, Gladiolus, Ixia, Watsonia, Sparaxis,* and *Freesia*. At about the same time, tuberous-rooted plants were introduced to Europe from North and South America. These included dahlias from Mexico and alstroemerias from Peru in 1789, and tigridia and the tuberose from Mexico around 1800.

Because bulbs are among the easiest plants to transport, they have been an important ingredient of American gardens since practically the time of earliest settlers. By the mid-1600s, Dutch settlers were established on Long Island and in New Jersey, where "each possessed a patch of cabbage and a bed of tulips." English settlers arriving in Virginia also brought in many bulbs. From these early times, there has been a two-way exchange of bulbs between Europe and North America. The dog-tooth violet (*Erythronium americanum*) and the Canadian lily (*Lilium canadense*) were among the earliest exports to Europe in the early 17th century. The orange cup lily (*L. philadelphicum*) and the Turk's cap lily (*L. superbum*) were two more important discoveries, but they did not reach European shores until 1737.

Over 65 genera of bulbs are listed in the Encyclopedia of Bulbs starting on page 82, and the history of each bulb is filled with hard work and sacrifice, triumph and rich rewards. Two with the most dramatic histories are the tulip and the iris. The costly and rare tulip has frequented royal courts and become the center of a world-wide, multimillion-dollar business. In contrast, the history of the iris takes place in the backyards and cottage gardens of amateurs and hobbyists. Around it has formed a large society of non-professional enthusiasts devoted solely to this flower.

The Tulip

From the time of its discovery, the tulip has been at various times surrounded with an aura of mystique, of rarity and expense, of jealousy and monopoly, of huge fortunes and big business. When tulips were first noted growing in Constantinople by Ogier Ghiselin de Busbecq, the famous Belgian diplomat and ambassador of the Holy Roman Empire, they were highly cultivated plants produced by much experimentation and development. In a letter dating from 1554, de Busbecq described this remarkable "new" flower and said, "The Turks cultivate the flowers with extreme zeal, and though they are careful people, do not hesitate to pay a considerable sum for an exceptional flower." The tulip probably had been cultivated for up to a thousand years prior to this time in the East, and by the time of de Busbecq's discovery it was the official flower of Sultan Suleiman's court. For decades after its importation into Europe, it was considered the symbol of the Ottoman Empire.

De Busbecq sent a few seeds and bulbs to Charles L'Escluse, then Prefect of the Royal Medicinal Garden in Prague. Apparently, L'Escluse did not quite understand the significance of this gift, and planted the bulbs in a heap. Later, he revealed that he'd been confused and had thought the tulip was some new form of vegetable. Accordingly, he gave 100 bulbs to a grocer in Vienna, who preserved them in sugar. And he reported that an Antwerp trader stewed his bulbs and ate them dressed with oil and vinegar!

Nevertheless, Europeans quickly discovered the beauty and value of this new flower, and its popularity began to spread. The Swiss botanist Gesner reported tulips growing in an Augsberg garden in 1559; L'Escluse himself sent a shipment to England in 1577, a year after making his discovery public. By 1582, tulips were being sold and exported at Haarlem in Holland. However, tulips were still relatively inexpensive at this point; a bill in the possession of the Marquis of Salisbury at Hatfield House in England shows this item: "tulip roots purchased at Haarlem at 10S. 100." Tulips reached Leiden in 1590, Belgium in 1593, Middleburgh in 1596, Montpelier in 1598, and Lucerne in 1599.

By the time L'Escluse left Vienna in 1593 and took the chair of botany at Leiden in Holland (taking his bulbs with him), the bulb craze was on the rise. Some claim that L'Escluse sold his bulbs for outrageous prices; others say that he would not part with the bulbs for any amount. In either case, a famous story relates that L'Escluse was pressed to sell his bulbs by some enterprising young traders who—unable to persuade the stubborn professor—sneaked into his garden one night and stole some. Disgusted, L'Escluse gave up his interest in tulips, never to grow them again.

Europe's imagination was fired by the virtually unlimited potential for newer and more exotic varieties (little-understood though they were).

Charles L'Escluse collected bulbs from the Near East for the Emperor Maximilian II and was instrumental in the spread of the tulip throughout Europe.

When grown from seed, tulips display an amazing variability and tendency to hybridize. Their susceptibility to certain viral diseases and genetic mutations further increases their variety, leading to "breaks" in color and to fantastic shapes. In 1597, the famous English botanist Gerard wrote of this profusion of tulip varieties, "all of which to describe particularlie, were to roule Sisiphus stone or numer the sandes." In 1629, John Parkinson described about 140 different varieties in *A Garden of All Sorts of Pleasant Flowers*, but noted that this number represented only a small percentage of the total. "Although I shall in this Chapter set down the varieties of a great many," he wrote, "I shall leave more unspoken of, than I shall describe; for I may well say, there is in this one plant no end of diversity to be expected, every year yielding a mixture and variety that hath not before been observed, and all this arising from the sowing of the seeds." He continues: "There are not only diverse kinds of Tulipas, but sundry diversities of colors in them, found out in these later days by many of the searchers of nature's varieties, which have not formerly been observed: our age being more delighted in the search, curiosity, and rarities of these pleasant delights than any age I think before."

Jan Breughel II (1601–1678) used monkeys to depict on canvas an allegory on the folly of the tulipomania of the 17th century. The group of monkeys on the veranda was meant to ridicule the tulip brokers' penchant for rich food and drink. (Courtesy Frans Hals Museum, Haarlem, Netherlands.)

By the 1620s, these "rarities of pleasant delights" had indeed become the playthings of the rich. In 1624, 'Semper Augustus', a tulip with red stripes against a white background, was selling for 1200 florins (the equivalent of about $1,600) *per bulb*. By 1625 the price had risen to over 3,000 florins. Some claimed that these fantastically high prices were started in France, where nobles of the court would pay up to 1,000 florins for a single bulb of an exceptional variety. Others maintain that the formation of the Dutch East India Trading Company in 1602 ushered in an unprecedented era of wealth in Holland, making the public ripe for speculative frenzy. In either case, the years 1634 to 1637 saw the amazing wave of speculation and gambling known as "tulipomania."

At first the bulbs were transported to Holland from Lille, in Flanders, where they were grown by monks. But eventually the auctions took place without the bulbs even being removed from the ground; instead they were sold by estimated weight. Bulbs changed hands many times, and each profitable transaction occurred without anyone actually *seeing* the bulbs involved. The mystique of tulips, previously limited to the rich alone, now spread to all classes as a new kind of currency and a high-pitched gambling fever. Small businesses were sold and the profits invested in bulbs. Property was traded, both real and personal. Many people went into debt at exorbitant interest rates. As the prices skyrocketed to phenomenal heights, so did the opportunity to make enormous profits. Who could pass up the

Flora's Wagon of Idiots, satirizing tulipomania, was painted by Hendrik Gerritszoon Pot (1585–1657). It was copied from an earlier engraving attributed to Chrispijn van de Passe. (Courtesy Frans Hals Museum, Haarlem, Netherlands.)

chance to earn as much as 60,000 florins (about $50,000) a month? In 1636, three bulbs of 'Semper Augustus' sold for 30,000 florins. A single bulb sold for 4,600 florins *and* a new carriage, a pair of dapple-gray horses, a sleigh with yet another horse, a painting of Judas, and a painting by Ruysdael. One story relates how a trader paid for a certain bulb with its weight in gold (15,000 florins), and then learned that a tradesman owned another bulb of the variety. The new owner then proceeded to destroy it before the shocked tradesman's eyes to ensure that his would remain the sole specimen. When he remarked that he would have paid ten times that amount, the distraught tradesman hanged himself.

The number of bulbs on the market has been estimated to have been around ten million, but few traders ever saw any of them. Because this wave of speculation was trading in something as insubstantial as the wind, it became known as the "wind trade" as well as tulipomania. And the bubble was destined to burst. The bottom finally fell out of the market in February 1637, when a group of traders simultaneously attempted to realize their paper holdings. Prices plummeted as spectacularly as they had risen, and much panic ensued as fortunes vanished. Laws were passed. Meetings among townships were held. But all to no avail. The "wind" had blown over.

When the prices fell to more normal levels and the craze had passed, the horticultural development of the bulb resumed a more rational course. While much of the varietal development took place in the original growing fields of Flanders, it was Holland that slowly built the tulip bulb into the industry it is today.

In Constantinople, the era of the tulip reached its zenith during the reign of Sultan Ahmed III (1703–30). During his reign, it was forbidden to buy or sell tulips outside the capital. Fachet, a French tulip merchant in Constantinople, once remarked that a tulip bulb was more highly valued than a human life. In 1726 it was estimated that there were at least a half-million bulbs in the Grand Vizier's gardens. Each year this was the scene of a lavish tulip festival, held by the light of a full moon. Hundreds of vases were arranged with the choicest varieties of tulips available, and set on stands decorated with crystal balls filled with colored water. Nightingales and canaries were in cages hung from the trees. Special crystal lamps illuminated the grand occasion. The guests were all required to wear colors that harmonized with the tulips.

During this period of Turkish history, known as "The Age of the Tulip," the oldest tulip book known was written: *Ferahengiz*. It included descriptions of 1,588 tulip varieties, each of which had to meet rigid standards in order to be included in the book. Possibly, this was the first time outside of the Orient official inspectors judged the merits of a flower by carefully enumerated standards for color, color patterns, size, and form. In the middle of the 18th century, Van Kampen published his *Dutch Florist*, establishing European criteria for excellence in tulips.

In the mid-19th century, Holland's tulip industry, by then an important part of the Dutch economy, began searching for wider markets. In 1849, Henrick Van der Shoot sailed to America, and spent nearly a year stumping the country. (From this trip, considered the maiden voyage of the Dutch bulb export industry, the tulip industry of Holland has grown to annual exports worth millions of dollars.) As business grew, the growers organized themselves into the Dutch Bulb Society (later called the Royal Dutch Bulb Society), and established a system of auctions, a code of ethics, and a court of arbitration to settle disputes.

Today, billions of tulips are grown and sold annually in the rich deltas of Holland, and this multimillion-dollar industry has become awesomely sophisticated and complex. The Dutch Bulb Center in Hillegom houses the Royal Dutch Bulb Society and its extensive library, the Court of Arbitration for the Bulb Trade, the Bulb Inspection Service, and the Council of Bulb Merchants—in addition to the large auction hall, where thousands of baskets of bulbs are traded daily. In the auction, buyers take their places at a numbered desk, each desk corresponding to a number alongside a large "clock" at the front of the hall. The numbers on the "clock" represent the bid price and starting at the high end the hand moves slowly downward. Sitting with their fingers poised on a button in the desk, the buyers push this button when the "clock" reaches a price they are willing to pay. The first to push the button buys the basket of bulbs. The pace moves at a dizzying speed; buyers must do their homework exceedingly well to be successful at this game.

In Lisse, an enormous complex houses the world-famous Laboratory for Bulb Research, a model of modern scientific facilities. Next to it is the State Horticultural School, where families in the bulb industry send their children to prepare to follow in their footsteps. Tulips have come a long way since that heap of bulbs in the corner of Charles L'Escluse's garden.

The Iris

Around the end of the 16th century, Charles L'Escluse described 28 different varieties of iris and then remarked that "a long experience has taught me that iris grown from seed vary in a wonderful way." John Gerard lists 16 varieties growing in his London garden in 1599. And 30 years later, John Parkinson described over 60 varieties. We know from these accounts and others that the iris was grown in many gardens through the 17th and 18th centuries—probably by being passed from gardener to gardener and over

Iris are longtime favorites in perennial borders. *Iris sibirica* in the foreground initiates the strong vertical effect of this planting.

backyard walls. Indeed, wild iris had been growing in European fields for centuries. A stylized version, the *fleur de lys*, had been used as a royal symbol by French kings since the 5th century. But not until the early 1800s did the formal history of the garden iris (the tall bearded iris) really begin.

In the early 19th century, De Bure, an amateur gardener in Paris, started selecting and naming the best of his iris varieties that arose from seed. A variety immodestly named after himself, 'Buriensis', was the first named iris introduced into commerce. De Bure encouraged the head gardener of the Royal Neuilly Domaine at Villers—a Monsieur Jacques—to grow more seedlings and begin introducing them to commerce. Jacques complied, and although he issued no catalog and gave no names to his seedlings, he did cause irises to become better known. In fact, he inspired a Monsieur Lémon of Belleville, France—a widely known nurseryman of his time—to specialize in iris. Lémon's catalogs went far and wide; by 1840 he offered 100 varieties for sale that he had named and raised himself; many of these were shipped as far away as California in various mixes. Up to this time, all iris varieties had been the result of bee pollination, and Lémon continued the tradition. When asked why he did not hand-pollinate, he said, "I am satisfied with the excellent results from mere chance, and doubt whether I would have done better by giving myself the trouble instead of leaving it to nature." Indeed, a few of these chance seedlings, such as the white and blue 'Mme. Chereu' and the white 'Innocenza', were still available in the catalogs of specialists as late as 1965.

Due to the popularity of Lémon's iris, competitors quickly appeared: Louis Van Houtte of Ghent, Victor and Verdier of Paris, and John Salter of England. Each offered seedlings of their own in an attempt to rival Lémon. In particular, John Salter followed Lémon's example and exported his rhizomes far and wide. By the 1880s, England had taken the lead in iris production, and the chief producer was the large nursery of Peter Barr of London. It is not known whether his varieties were pollinated by bees or by human hands. The first documented hand crosses were made in the 1890s—by Amos Perry and George Reuth in England, and by Goos and Koenemann in Germany. These varieties were considered to be so fine that most growers believed that further improvement was impossible. And once again, in the tradition of De Bure, it was an amateur who changed the course of history.

Iris 'Dazzling Gold', a bearded hybrid, is among the diverse varieties of iris available—many developed by amateur gardeners.

Michael Foster (later knighted) a professor of physiology at Cambridge, enjoyed gardening as a hobby, and was particularly fascinated by the iris. He grew virtually every known species in his garden, and was constantly breeding and selecting varieties. Like other iris lovers of his day, he too despaired of further improvement unless new genetic material could be introduced. He had missionaries and merchant contacts in the Near East on the lookout for new irises, and many previously unknown species were being sent to him. The crosses he subsequently made were to revolutionize irises, and make the tall bearded iris the magnificent flower it is today. Foster is currently recognized as the father of the modern iris.

In the United States, several other "amateurs" dramatically advanced the history of the iris, notably Bertrand H. Farr and Frank X. Schreiner. In the late 1890s, Bertrand H. Farr, then a music store owner in Reading, Pennsylvania, and an avid amateur gardener, received a catalog from the nurseries of Peter Barr in London. He was so excited over the beautiful iris listed that he purchased all the varieties offered—over 100 of them—and started a nursery in the nearby town of Wyoming. Growing a huge number of seedlings bred from this stock, he published a lavish color catalog in 1905, featuring many that he had named and introduced. In spite of his outrageous price (50¢ apiece), his plants were met with great acclaim. Farr is credited with giving an enormous boost to iris popularity in this country, along with raising many top-class varieties.

Like Farr, Frank X. Schreiner was a dedicated amateur who decided, following Emerson's advice, to "first find your hobby, then make it your profession." Affer his doctors advised him to give up the indoor work of managing a department of a large store, he started a nursery. Under the influence of John Wister, the first president of the American Iris Society, he began specializing in iris. Although Schreiner did not breed and introduce new varieties himself, his sons did, and they are in the forefront of iris hybridizing to this day. One of Schreiner's greatest contributions, however, was the annual list he published in his catalog of what he considered to be the 100 best irises available. Noted for its objective criteria and sound plantsmanship, this list became a tradition eventually assumed by the American Iris Society. Each year the Society publishes an annual list of the 100 best irises, as determined by mail polls of its members.

The American Iris Society was formed in 1920, with John Wister of Swarthmore, Pennsylvania, as its first president. In addition to its annual poll, every ten years the society publishes a checklist of all new varieties registered from around the world. Serving as a fulcrum of contact for iris enthusiasts everywhere, it has thousands of members.

Banks of clivias lend their warm color to the soft greenery of a southern garden.

TYPES OF BULBS

Not all "bulbs" are true bulbs. Corms, rhizomes, tubers, and tuberous roots are also called bulbs.

Most people consider any plant a bulb if it stores energy in an underground fleshy organ during the dormant period of its life. However, only some of these plants are true bulbs. These subterranean storage forms have differences as well as similarities.

The common factor of the various bulbous plants is their ability to store food on which they can live during a period of adverse weather conditions until they can start growing above ground again. Natural causes may produce this "dormancy"—for example, winter or drought. But in mild climates, it may be necessary to induce dormancy by withholding moisture or removing the bulbs from the ground for a period of artificial cold storage.

True Bulbs

Only about half the plants described in this book are grown from true bulbs. Inside a true bulb is a tiny, fully formed plant encased within fleshy scales. If you slice vertically through a tulip bulb at planting time (October), you will see a miniature plant—complete with tiny flower buds, stem, and leaves that have been forming all through summer.

The scales surrounding the embryo are modified leaves. These contain all the foods needed to sustain the bulb during dormancy and early growth. The scales may be loose and open, like those of a lily, or tight and compact, like those of an onion. If a tight bulb is cut in half crosswise, the scales look like rings.

Around the scales, many bulbs have a paper-thin covering known as the *tunic* (as in onions). At the bottom of the bulb is a modified stem, or *basal plate,* from which the roots emerge. This basal plate also holds the scales together. During the growing season, new bulbs (called *bulblets* or *offsets*) are formed from lateral buds on the basal plate. In some bulbs, such as the tulip, the old bulb dies, leaving only the new ones. In other bulbs, such as the narcissus, the parent continues to grow, and the bulblets can be separated from it to create new plants. A few bulbs (lilies, for example) form new *bulbils* in the leaf axis.

Corms

A corm is actually a stem that is modified into a mass of storage tissue. If you cut a corm in half crosswise, you won't see any rings. The top of the corm has one or more growing points—"eyes"—which usually are visible if you look closely. Corms are covered by dry leaf bases that resemble the tunic covering many bulbs. There are no enlarged scales. Roots grow from a basal plate on the underside of the corm. As the plant grows, the corm shrivels away. New corms form on top of or next to the old one. In addition, some corms, such as gladiolus, form small *cormels* (tiny corms) around the base plate or roots. Large corms produce flowers the following year, but cormels take from two to three years to develop sufficiently to bloom.

Daffodils spring from true bulbs, which, if allowed to naturalize, will form masses of flowers.

Tubers

The underground tuber is a solid mass of stem. While similar to the corm, it lacks both a basal plate and the corm's tunic-like covering. Roots and shoots grow from growth buds (eyes) scattered over the surface. As the plants grow, some tubers, such as potatoes, diminish in size and form new tubers; others, such as ranunculus, increase in size as they store nutrients and develop new growth buds for the following year.

Tuberous Roots

These nutrient-storage units look like tubers, but are really swollen roots rather than stems. During growth, they produce fibrous roots that take in moisture and nutrients. New growth buds appear on the base of the old stem, at the point where it joined the tuberous root. Roots such as dahlias can be divided by cutting off a section that still has an eye-bearing portion of the old stem attached.

Rhizomes

Sometimes known as *rootstock*, rhizomes are actually thickened, branching storage stems. They grow laterally just along or slightly below the surface of the soil. Roots develop on the lower surface; buds growing along the top of the rhizome produce the new plants during the growing season. Rhizomatous plants, such as bearded irises, may be propagated by cutting the parent into sections, making sure that each segment contains a growth bud. Other rhizomatous plants, such as lilies-of-the-valley (*Convallaria majalis*), are propagated from underground rootstalks, or shoots, called *pips*.

True Bulbs

Bulbs are composed of modified leaves. The individual leaves are seen as scales (as in lilies) or rings (as in narcissus and tulips).

Types of True Bulbs

Allium
Amaryllis
Camassia
Chinodoxa
Clivia
Eucharis
Fritillaria
Galanthus
Hippeastrum
Hyacinthus
Hymenocallis
Iris (bulbous)
Ixiolirion
Leucojum
Lilium
Lycoris
Muscari
Narcissus
Nerine
Ornithogalum
Oxalis
Scilla
Sprekelia
Tulipa
Zephyranthes

From left to right: narcissus (this one is a *double-nosed* bulb), lily, tulip.

Bulbils on a lily stem.

Corms

Corms are composed of modified stem tissue. They have no rings or scales.

Types of Corms

Brodiaea
Bulbocodium
Colchicum
Crocus
Erythronium
Freesia
Gladiolus
Ixia
Moraea
Sparaxis
Tigridia
Tritonia
Watsonia

Tubers

Like corms, tubers are developed from stem tissue.

Types of Tubers

Anemone
Caladium
Cyclamen
Eranthis
Gloriosa
Polianthes
Ranunculus
Sinningia

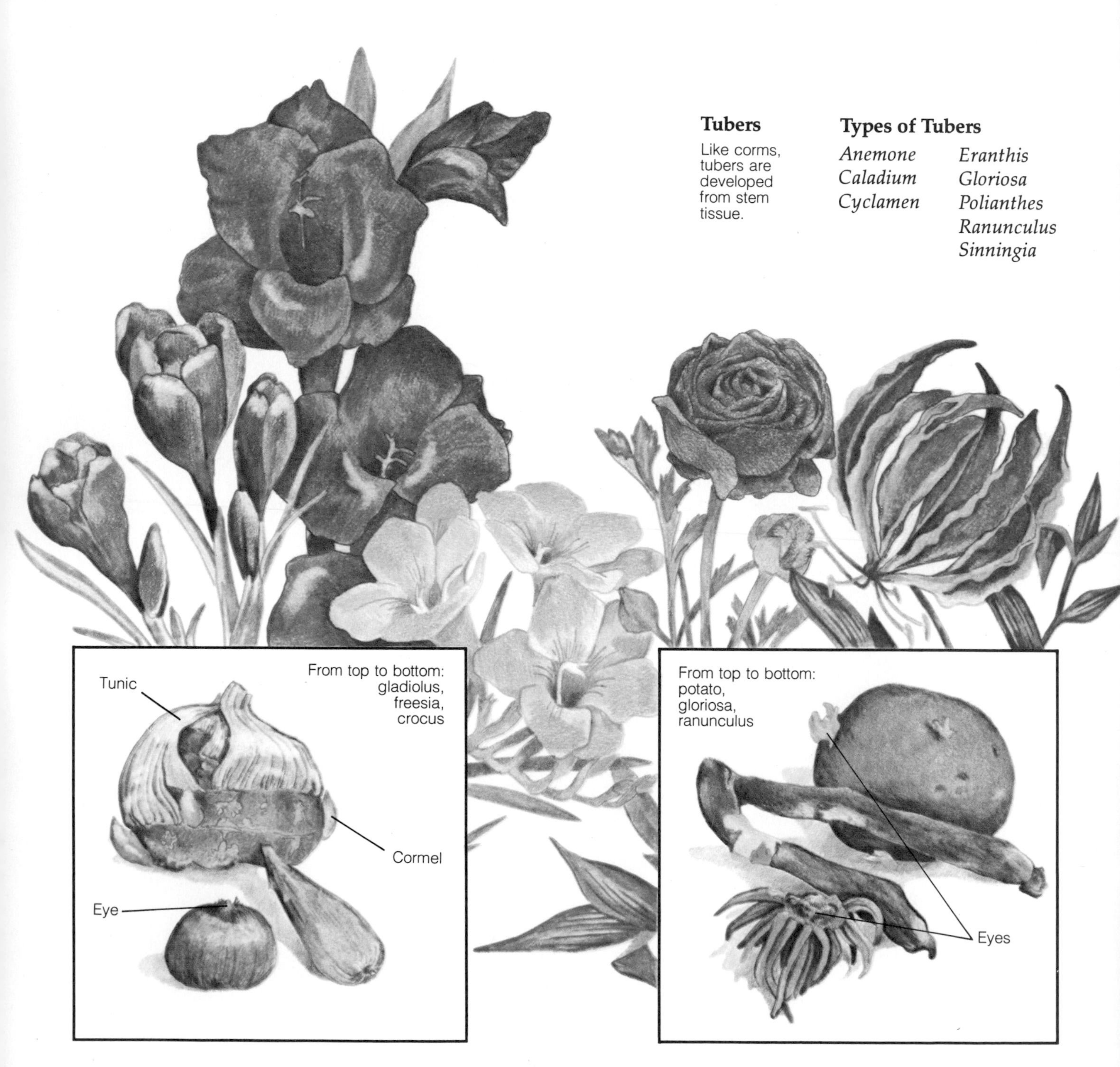

From top to bottom: gladiolus, freesia, crocus

From top to bottom: potato, gloriosa, ranunculus

Tuberous Roots

These look like tubers, but are developed from root tissue.

Types of Tuberous Roots

Alstroemeria
Begonia
Dahlia
Eremurus

Rhizomes

These are horizontal stems or runners.

Types of Rhizomes

Achimenes
Agapanthus
Canna
Convallaria
Iris (rhizomatous)
Zantedeschia

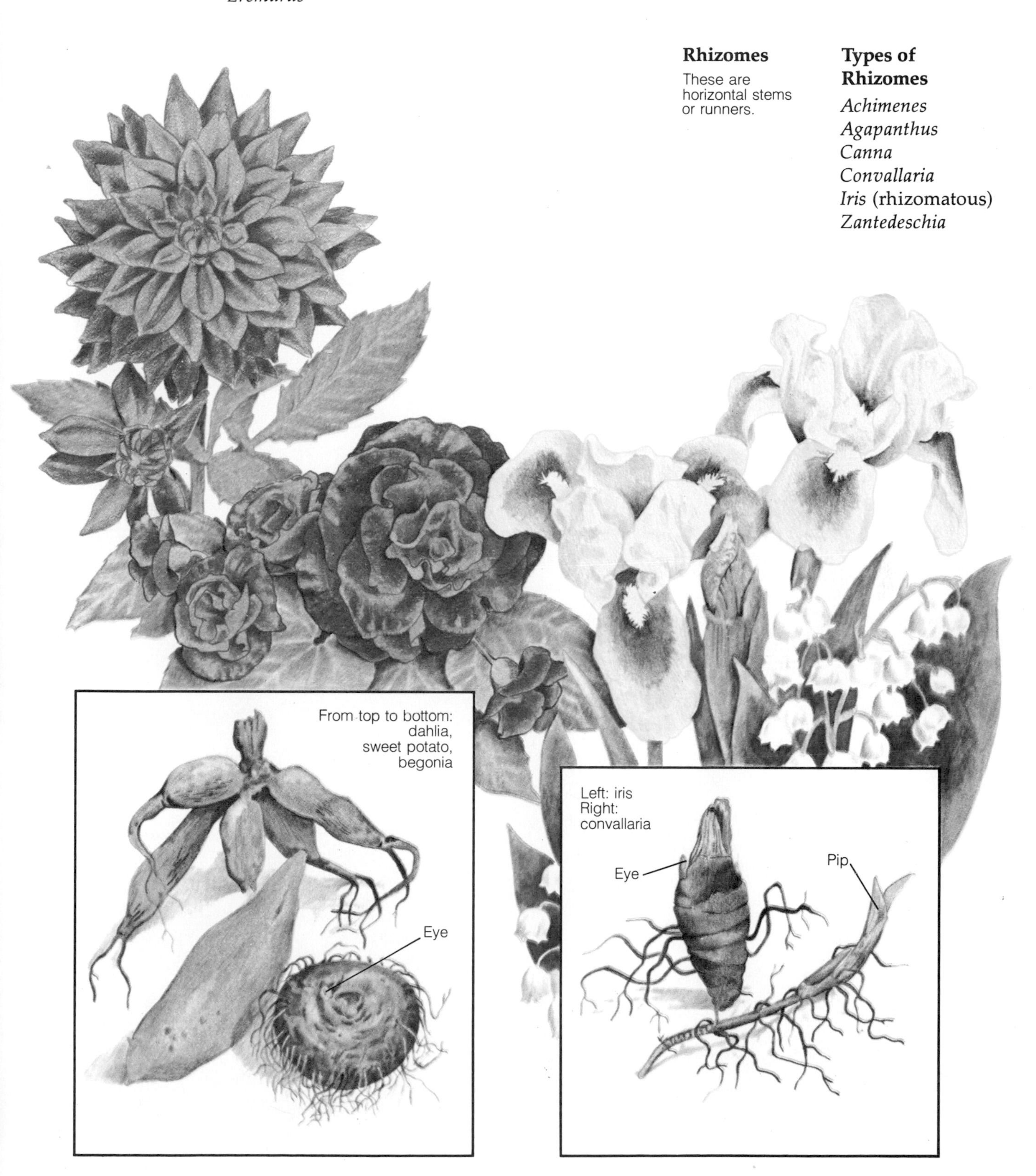

From top to bottom: dahlia, sweet potato, begonia

Left: iris
Right: convallaria

The Bulb Industry

You already know about the Dutch tulip industry, but the general bulb industry is also a professional and thriving business. Each year, billions of bulbs are produced and sold. The Netherlands leads the way in modern bulb production, with England, the United States, and Japan following closely behind.

Bulb producers are not content simply to multiply the same tried-and-true bulbs for their markets. They strive both to produce new bulb varieties and to improve existing ones through the latest scientific methods.

In the Dutch bulb industry, for example, hybridization and scientific research are conducted with an intensity that is causing tremendous changes in home gardens. Since the 17th century, growers in the world's bulb capitals have used a combination of science, experience, and luck to hybridize new tulip, narcissus, and other bulb varieties.

Countless new varieties have been produced by several generations of a few Dutch families who have cross-pollinated flowers and nursed their progeny. This time-consuming process involves removing pollen-producing stamens from one variety and brushing them against the pollen-receptive stigma of another variety. Out of thousands of crosses, perhaps only one new variety may be deemed superior to existing varieties.

Bulbs in a Dutch field are being raised for the world market.

Bulb displays give the gardener an opportunity to evaluate new varieties.

Once a new flower has been selected, it may take as long as 10 to 15 years for the original parent to produce enough bulbs so that the new variety can be presented to the Dutch Bulb Jury. It is the awesome task of this jury, which meets each Monday at the Bloembollencentrum (Flower-Bulb Center) in Hillegom, to decide which varieties are worthy of being introduced. This stamp of approval allows the producers to develop enough bulbs for sale in the marketplace a few years later, thus rewarding all their efforts with satisfaction as well as money. Unless the jurors approve the variety, all the work involved adds up to a pretty flower that will be seen by only a few people. The complexity of creating new bulb varieties justifies the high prices that must be charged for new flowers. Then, as propagation makes more bulbs available, the prices begin to fall.

A number of bulb producers in the Netherlands are currently experimenting with different scientifically controlled methods of producing new plants other than hybridizing. The Institute for Horticultural Plant Breeding is exposing bulbs to: virus-carrying aphids under highly controlled conditions; nitrous oxide, to alter the genetic makeup of the parent bulb; and X-rays, to create mutations. These unorthodox methods have produced original-looking flowers at a much faster rate than have the time-honored approaches. But in spite of these experiments, most Dutch bulb producers still credit old-fashioned luck and keen observation as the secret of the most beautiful new hybrids.

In the United States, University of California botanists are at work on improving strains of the Peruvian lily (*Alstroemeria*), the calla lily (*Zantedeschia*), the peacock iris (*Moraea*), the tuberous begonia, and other bulbs that can be grown in home gardens everywhere. Coast to coast, State Agricultural Experiment Stations and botanical gardens are growing the new bulbs for evaluation.

In addition to introducing new flowers that appear annually at garden centers and in catalogs, growers everywhere are experimenting with techniques for developing bulbs that prove hardier in cold climates. As a result, some lilies and gladioli can remain in the ground all year round in all but the coldest climates.These experiments have produced colors and hues that were unheard of 25 years ago, as well as flowers that last longer, both on the stem and when cut. Bearded irises that produce a second crop of blossoms in the fall have recently been introduced. Bulbs with larger, exhibition-sized blooms are now offered, as well as miniature varieties of traditional full-

Opposite: Daffodils break through winter leaves and blend into a natural setting.

Right: The true bulb forms new bulbs during the growing season. The pregnant onion (*Ornithogalum caudatum*) provides a dramatic, above-ground display of this process.

Below: A lily pollinated by a hybridizer is being protected from further pollination by a bag over the stigma.

sized plants. New developments continue to give more fragrance and other desirable qualities in all the plants classified as bulbs.

The world bulb industry is very much alive and heading in new directions, all destined to provide home gardeners with bulbs of quality that will increase the rewards of bulb gardening.

Looking Ahead

It has been said that no landscape is complete without the inclusion of some bulbs. The next chapter offers some fresh ideas for incorporating bulbs into your existing or planned landscape design.

Bulbs are usually associated with springtime, but actually there are bulbs for every season, including indoor winter blooms. The fourth chapter, beginning on page 46, includes suggestions for creating your personal calendar of year-round bulb enjoyment.

The basics of bulb gardening are simple, compared with some other gardening tasks, and most bulbs share common cultural techniques. On page 64 you'll find out how to grow healthy plants from your bulb investment. First come tips for recognizing healthy bulbs. Then you learn how to select and prepare the site, how to plant and maintain bulbs throughout their growing cycle, and finally, how to harvest and store them safely for another year.

More than 3,000 species of bulbs flourish all over the world. The Encyclopedia of Bulbs on page 82 offers information about bulbs that are best for home gardens. All the familiar bulbs are there, as well as a few of the more unusual ones to help you add a touch of drama to your garden.

A well-planned informal garden displays spring color with beds of bulbs.

GARDENING WITH BULBS

The effects of various colors and combinations of bulbs in the landscape can be breathtaking when massed or quietly pleasing when naturalized.

Bulbs add a unique element to the garden that other plant forms cannot. Consider the stately elegance of lilies in summer, or the delicate subtlety of lilies-of-the-valley in spring. The first crocus or glory-of-the-snow lends a lively look to the landscape; so does the fall-flowering crocus. What would formal gardens be without beds of tulips or hyacinths? Can you imagine informal cottage gardens without clumps of daffodils? And brightly colored alliums, dahlias, gladioli, and lilies give visual highlights to the garden in summer.

But bulbs can also be used to create a soothing effect as well as a lively one. You can plant delicate pastels that harmonize together; a collection of all-white flowering bulbs can fill a garden spot with its sparkling-clean beauty. No landscape seems complete without bulbs. Flowers need not be merely decorations in the garden, but should be considered as basic elements of your overall design. Once you know what you want to do with your personal landscape, then you are ready to select the plants that will accomplish your goals. In many instances, bulbs will do the trick, either planted by themselves or mixed with other flowers.

As you think about incorporating bulbs into your existing or proposed landscape plan, collect ideas from all available sources. Using magazines and garden catalogs, clip out appealing photographs of individual bulbs as well as attractive plantings. To give you further ideas, this chapter presents planting suggestions and color combinations from many public and private gardens.

Bulbs in the Home Landscape

When planning your landscape, consider these ideas from gardens around the world.

- ☐ Be selective. Your garden will look more dynamic if you concentrate on only a few kinds of bulbs rather than set out many different types.
- ☐ Bulbs look best when planted in drifts or clumps rather than as isolated plants or in single rows.
- ☐ When planting bulbs in clumps in a border or bed, avoid a spotty pattern: group them so that each bulb's foliage will gradually merge into the next.
- ☐ Consider planting in free-flowing arcs, rather than restricting yourself to rigid rows or formal geometric shapes.
- ☐ To add interest to flower beds, vegetable gardens, or the front of shrub groupings, plant borders of low-growing bulbs such as hyacinth, muscari, or small narcissus.
- ☐ Plant annual or wildflower seeds along with bulbs, or set out annual transplants as the bulbs begin to fade. This helps hide the bulbs' ripening yellow foliage (which must not be removed because it allows the bulbs to accumulate the food necessary to carry them through dormancy).

The perennial edging of candytuft will help conceal the ripening foliage of the tulips.

☐ If you want the look of estate formality, choose tulips, irises, hyacinths, anemones, or ranunculuses. These are spectacular when planted in large blocks of a single variety or grouped by color to create patterned designs. Delicately flowered bulbs are less effective in such formal plantings.

☐ If you want to plant bulbs to create patterns or color combinations, carefully read the descriptions in catalogs or on labels in order to select those that will bloom at the same time.

☐ Spring-flowering bulbs look wonderful combined with pansies, violas, primroses, alyssum, or other flowers. Similar effects can be achieved by planting summer-flowering bulbs along with nasturtium, miniature zinnias, phlox, marigolds, and other annuals.

☐ In an English cottage garden, combine bulbs with shrubs, perennials, annuals, and wildflowers for a long succession of flowers. Set out bulbs in large drifts. However, plant lilies, callas, crown imperials, fritillarias, and other large bulbs as occasional accents.

☐ To break up expanses of green lawn, create lush areas of color by planting bulbs of one type or color, or of mixed hues, that are compatible with your garden design.

☐ Highlight a lawn with an edging of colorful bulbs. As a frame sets off a picture, a border adds a distinctive finishing touch.

☐ Plant clumps of fragrant bulbs near entryways or open windows to make the most of their perfume.

☐ Plant a fragrance garden of hyacinth, narcissus, lily-of-the-valley, or other perfumed bulbs. Place the bulbs so you can sit or rest near the flowers, or plant them beside your favorite backyard picnic area.

☐ Remove a section of paving from the patio, driveway, or sidewalk, and fill the dirt with a clump of colorful bulbs.

☐ Line walkways and paths with bulbs to invite exploration of the rest of the garden.

☐ Plant bulbs in raised or recessed beds built into patios or terraces. This brings the flowers and their fragrances into the outdoor entertainment area.

☐ Position bulbs where you can see them from inside the house as you dine or relax.

☐ To create a wall or bank of color, set out terraced plantings of bulbs combined with annuals on a steep hillside or slope.

☐ When planting ground covers, include bulbs that are hardy in your area and can naturalize. They will provide colorful additions to the green groundcover. Check the following chapter for bulbs that bloom at different seasons, and plant spring, summer, and fall types for a succession of color.

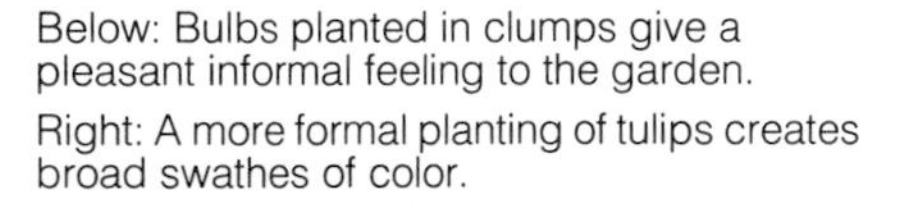

Below: Bulbs planted in clumps give a pleasant informal feeling to the garden.

Right: A more formal planting of tulips creates broad swathes of color.

Left: White *Lilium testaceum* in the gardens of Sissinghurst Castle in England provide a vertical accent above a bed of low-growing *Alchemilla mollis*, as well as a visual transition to the spires of delphiniums in the background.

Below: Yellow tulips lead the march of colorful pansies up this terraced hillside.

Bottom right: Colorful ranunculus make a vivid border for a lawn.

Bottom left: Tulips combine with spring-blooming azaleas and rhododendrons in contrasting hues in London's Kensington Gardens.

Above: Bulbs brighten the annual Chelsea flower show in London.

Below: Old Westbury Gardens on Long Island, New York, displays mass plantings of tulips.

Bulb Displays

Public gardens with bulb displays are some of the best places to find out which specific bulbs you want to grow. When you see a flower you like, look at the label and note the name. These gardens are also a good source of planting ideas and color combinations you can use at home

The most magnificent bulb displays can be found in two public gardens: at Keukenhof in the Netherlands, operated by the Netherlands Flower-Bulb Institute; and at Springfields in Spalding, Lincolnshire, England. If you are planning to travel to these areas in spring, be sure to include visits to these gardens.

Other impressive bulb displays are on view in public parks and famous gardens, such as Longwood Gardens in Pennsylvania, Butchart Gardens in British Columbia, Old Westbury Gardens on Long Island, and Winterthur in Delaware. Planting Fields Arboretum in Oyster Bay, New York, has a fine display of naturalized bulbs. You can view late-summer displays of tuberous begonias at the Conservatory in San Francisco's Golden Gate Park, as well as in the greenhouses of nearby bulb growers in Santa Cruz and Capitola.

Flower shows, both local and international, are great places to glean ideas. The annual Chelsea Flower Show in London has magnificent bulb displays each spring, and the pinnacle of flower shows is the World Flower Show, held in Amsterdam every 10 years.

Top left: The annual bulb show at Keukenhof in the Netherlands is one of the most famous in the world.

Top right: Begonias on display at the Conservatory in San Francisco's Golden Gate Park.

Center right: Spring bulbs grace the formal garden at Hampton Court Palace in England.

Middle: New varieties of narcissus are displayed at the annual Chelsea flower show in London.

Center left: Tulips at Longwood Gardens in Pennsylvania.

Bottom: Bulbs with large blossoms, such as hyacinths, lend themselves to a formal design.

Opposite: An all-white theme creates a mood of serenity and spaciousness. White daisies interplanted with the tulips will continue the theme after the tulips have faded.

Right: The brillant red-orange of these tulips are planted to good advantage against a contrasting dark fence.

Below right: This monochromatic design combines tulips and hyacinths in similar shades.

Below: The warm tones of lilies and evening primroses complement one another to create a unified design.

Bottom: The contrasting colors of these daffodils and violas add definition to the planting bed.

Color in the Garden

Bulbs offer a varied choice of color schemes. Many people prefer to blend all bulb flowers in a riot of colors; others prefer a more carefully worked out plan that eliminates clashing colors and creates a more harmonious effect. It is really a matter of personal preference.

You can create a monochromatic scheme by selecting bulbs that bloom in a single color or several shades of that color. Nothing is more relaxing or romantic than the all-white garden. Bulbs also lend themselves to the all-blue garden; to pink, peach, and salmon hues; to golden yellows; to brilliant reds; or to purples and lavenders only.

Above: Accents of red and blue emphasize rather than detract from the pink theme of a mixed border.

Above right: Yellow daffodils stand out against the light bark of a sycamore.

You may prefer carefully worked out blends of two or three colors with such shades as yellows and oranges planted together, or only pinks and reds. Or you may choose two contrasting colors, such as lavenders with oranges, or yellows and blues.

Mixed colors need space. If you have lots of room, use bold splashes of bulb color in many hues. White flowers interspersed here and there tend to blend such plantings. In smaller areas, however, mixed colors lose their effectiveness, so use only pastels or fewer colors.

Bright, warm colors planted at the rear of a garden make the space appear smaller and closer; cool colors or white make the garden appear longer or deeper.

Most bulb flowers show up best against a background of dark green foliage or against a dark painted fence or wall. However, the deep purple or dark-red tones of many tulips and other bulbs need a light-colored background in order to show off their rich coloration to the best advantage.

Whatever color scheme you choose to live with, plan your plantings so that you can enjoy color on many levels. Use tall-growing lilies, gladioli, or tulips for height, along with lower growing plants, to achieve blooms on several levels.

The following color specifics may give you additional planting guidelines:

Red and yellow tulips and blue violas contrast strongly with one another.

- ☐ Plant a patch of yellow daffodils against a background of white-barked birch or sycamore trees.
- ☐ Blue muscari looks stunning planted around yellow forsythia.
- ☐ Plant white daffodils among blue forget-me-nots.
- ☐ Carpet the ground around pink azaleas with white chionodoxa.
- ☐ Mixed yellow daffodils seem quite at home under flowering fruit trees; plant all-white trumpet daffodils beneath white dogwoods and white-flowering fruit trees.
- ☐ Blue flowers have a magical, fairy-tale quality. For an all-blue garden combine *Iris reticulata, Anemone blanda, Muscari* species, *Scilla siberica, Chionodoxa luciliae,* and *Camassia quamash* with blue hyacinths, blue cultivars of Dutch iris, and other blue-flowering bulbs. Include some delphinium and forget-me-nots.
- ☐ Bed purple and white tulips in front of purple-and-white magnolias.
- ☐ Plan something unexpected for the summer landscape; plant masses of green gladioli blended with green zinnias.
- ☐ Lighter colors (whites and yellows) stand out at dusk, while the darker colors (reds and blues) disappear.

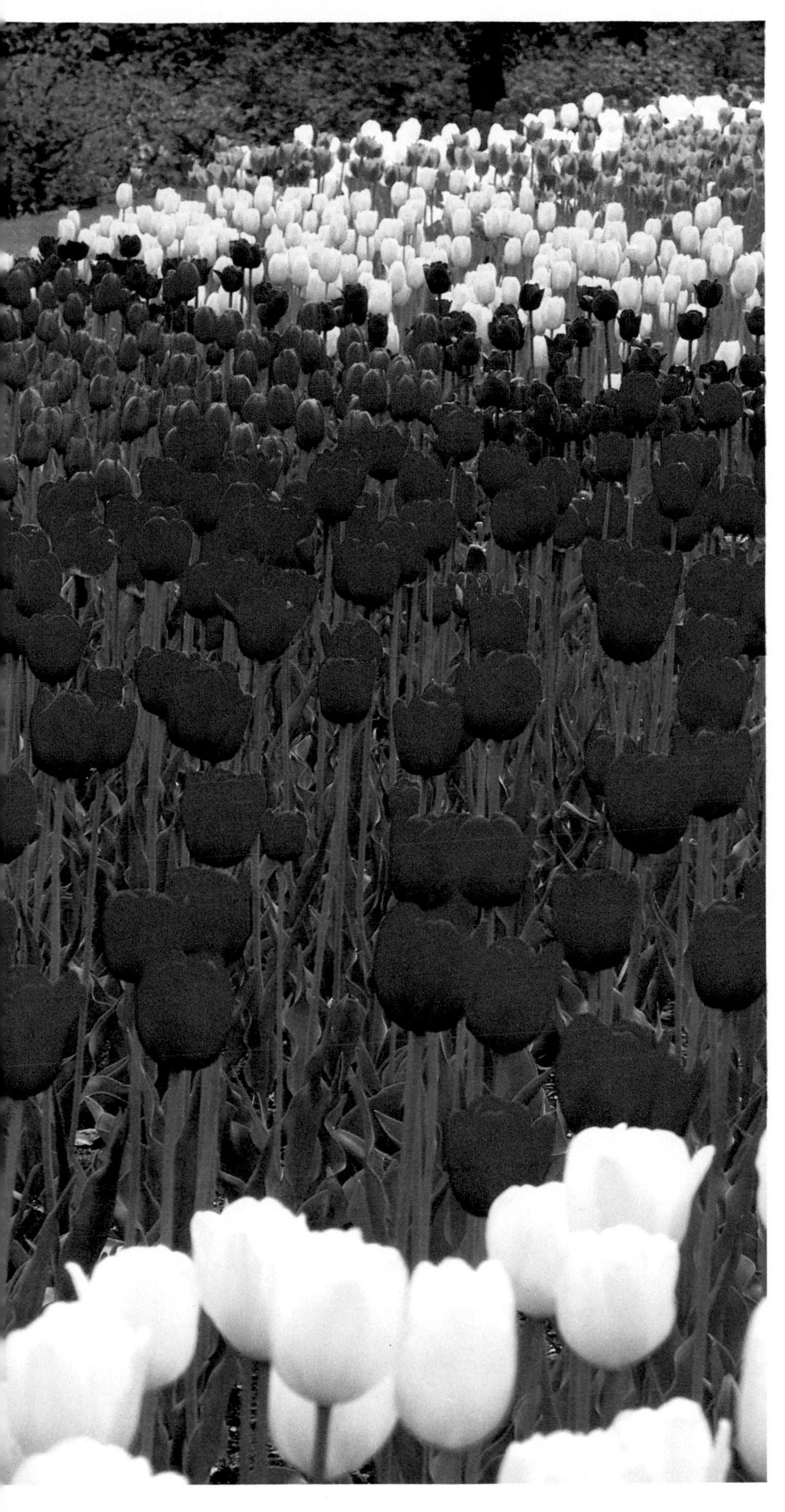

Deep contrasting colors in large blocks make a strong statement in a mass planting.

Random clumps of naturalized daffodils provide color over a large area (top) and a mass planting provides a brilliant sweep of color in a grassy dale (below).

Naturalized Landscapes

A naturalized landscape is one that seems to have come about on its own, without human interference. Bulbs are especially effective in this kind of setting. Usually, you need considerable space and many bulbs, but you can also get good results with only a few dozen bulbs in limited space, such as underneath a tree.

Naturalized bulbs look wonderful on a grassy bank, in the corner of a large lawn, spilling over from an adjoining field, along a country fence, or filling a wooded glade.

Naturalized bulbs can be left undisturbed for years. However, eventually they may become overcrowded. If so, dig them up and separate the bulbs. But if your initial planting of the bulbs goes a bit deeper than normally recommended, they will divide more slowly, thus delaying the time when they must be separated.

For a natural look, don't formulate a planting plan and lay out the bulbs accordingly. Instead, scatter the bulbs randomly over the planting area by hand and then plant them where they fall.

Lavender muscari blend well with pink flowers and leaves in this naturalized bed.

Bulbs for Naturalizing

Allium species
Amaryllis belladonna
Anemone blanda
A. apennina
Brodiaea laxa
Camassia
Chionodoxa
Colchicum
Crocus
Cyclamen (Hardy)
Eranthis
Erythronium
Fritillaria meleagris
Galanthus
Iris reticulata
Leucojum
Lilium tigrinum
Muscari species
Narcissus
Ornithogalum nutans
O. umbellatum
Scilla
Tulipa clusiana
T. kaufmanniana hybrids,
T. tarda

Gardening in Miniature

A number of the smaller or miniature bulbs are ideally suited to rock or alpine gardens. Plant clusters of 3 or more bulbs in crevices. Some bulbs spread rapidly, such as colchicum and muscari. Place these where they have room to expand and where their foliage does not crowd out smaller plants.

When making your plant selections, remember that a rock garden is usually informal, so consider using only one or two specimens of many different kinds of bulbs. As well as offering aesthetic pleasure, this scheme will allow you to observe how particular bulbs grow.

Bulbs for Rock or Other Miniature Gardens

Allium karataviense
Anemone coronaria 'St. Brigid'; also
A. apennina
A. blanda
A. fulgens
A. palmata
Brodiaea laxa
Bulbocodium vernum
Chionodoxa
Crocus
Eranthis hyemalis
Erythronium albidum
E. americanum
E. oregonum 'White Beauty'
Hyacinthus
Dwarf iris, including:
Iris bakerana
I. danfordiae
I. histrioides
I. reticulata
Leucojum aestivum
L. vernum
Moraea pavonia 'Magnifica'
Muscari
Dwarf narcissus, including:
Narcissus minimus
N. bulbocodium
N. nana
Oxalis adenophylla
Scilla siberica
S. tubergeniana
S. bifolia
Sparaxis tricolor
Zantedeschia

In the right setting, a single clump of bulbs, such as these spring snowflakes (*Leucojum vernum*), can be a miniature garden.

A bowl of hyacinths can be grown to the flowering stage in an out-of-the-way place and then moved to a place of prominence.

Containerized Landscapes

Many bulbs adapt particularly well to container gardening. When you grow bulbs in pots and other containers, you can bring them indoors at the peak of their bloom or enjoy them on the patio.

Container-grown bulbs can be moved about at whim to create instant landscape changes. Sink them in flower beds to add color; group them at an entrance to welcome visitors; position them outdoors where they can be enjoyed from inside; or bring them near an outdoor eating area to enhance your dining pleasure.

However, bulbs—like other plants—are less hardy when planted in containers than when planted in the ground. So to protect them in winter, place the pots in a trench and cover them with straw, or move them to a protected location. For more instructions on caring for bulbs in containers, see page 68.

In addition, bulbs planted in pots can be "forced," or brought into bloom out of season, if given conditions that bring them out of dormancy. See page 57 for forcing techniques.

These pots of tulips transform a sunny porch into a conservatory.

Bulbs for Containers

Achimenes
Agapanthus
Allium (short types)
Anemone blanda
Begonia
Caladium
Chionodoxa
Clivia
Crocus
Cyclamen
Eranthis
Eucharis
Freesia
Gladiolus (miniature)
Hippeastrum
Hyacinthus
Iris danfordiae
I. histrioides
I. reticulata
Lilium
Muscari
Narcissus
Nerine
Ornithogalum
Oxalis
Polianthes
Sinningia
Tulipa (early or midseason varieties)
Zantedeschia

Bulbs can be "forced," or brought into bloom before their normal season, to brighten a windowsill during winter.

BULBS FOR ALL SEASONS

Most people think of bulbs as spring flowers, but by planting the right bulbs at the right time, you can have flowers in summer, fall, and winter as well.

The word "bulbs" may suggest tulips, narcissus, and hyacinths in the spring. But you're in for a surprise as well as a treat: bulbs can also be grown in summer, fall, and winter. True, bulbous plants do appear at the onset of spring, beginning the annual progression of flowers through the gardening year.

But the outdoor garden can be filled, or at least accented, with bulbs from the last days of winter right on through fall, not just in spring. By planting the appropriate bulbs at the appropriate time, you can extend the flowering season to bring you delight every day of the year. Each season offers its own specialties.

In early spring, for example, you can treat yourself to any or all of the following: *Anemone, Bulbocodium, Chionodoxa, Crocus, Cyclamen* (hardy), *Eranthis, Galanthus, Iris, Leucojum, Narcissus, Oxalis, Ranunculus, Scilla,* and *Zephyranthes*.

In spring, try: *Achimenes, Agapanthus, Allium, Anemone, Brodiaea, Caladium, Calochortus, Camassia, Convallaria, Eremurus, Fritillaria, Gladiolus, Hymenocallis, Iris, Ixia, Ixiolirion, Muscari, Narcissus, Ornithogalum, Oxalis, Ranunculus, Scilla, Tulipa,* and *Zephyranthes*.

In summer, there's: *Achimenes, Agapanthus, Allium, Alstroemeria, Begonia, Brodiaea, Caladium, Calochortus, Camassia, Canna, Dahlia, Gladiolus, Lilium, Oxalis, Ranunculus, Tigridia, Tritonia, Watsonia,* and *Zephyranthes*.

In late summer and fall, perk yourself up with: *Achimenes, Agapanthus, Allium, Amaryllis, Begonia, Canna, Colchicum, Cyclamen* (hardy), *Dahlia, Gladiolus, Leucojum, Lilium, Lycoris, Nerine, Oxalis, Polianthes,* and *Zephyranthes*.

And finally, brighten up winter with: *Convallaria, Crocus, Cyclamen* (hardy), *Freesia, Hippeastrum, Hyacinthus, Leucojum aestivum, Moraea, Oxalis,* and *Zephyranthes*.

Bulbs can also be grown indoors as houseplants. A well-placed container of bulbous flowers can do much to brighten a gloomy winter. Any bulb that flowers naturally in hot summers or is a native of a hot climate is likely to thrive when used as a houseplant. (Just be sure to keep it away from direct contact with hot air, such as air from a radiator or heating vent.) Good choices include *Achimenes* (it blooms from spring through late fall), *Agapanthus* (summer–late fall), *Clivia* (spring), *Cyclamen persicum* (late summer–early spring), *Eucharis* (year-round), *Freesia* (winter–early spring), *Gloriosa* (summer–late fall), *Hippeastrum* (winter–early spring), *Hyacinthus* (winter–spring), *Moraea* (year-round), *Narcissus* (winter–early spring), *Sinningia* (year-round), *Sparaxis* (spring), *Sprekelia* (spring), and *Zantedeschia* (year-round).

To bring hardy spring bulbs into early bloom, the process called "forcing"—making a bulb bloom at an unnatural time or under unnatural conditions—can be used to duplicate nature's cooling period. Forcing can

give you early potted glories or early cut flowers. And the greenhouse, for the fortunate gardener who has one, will widen your botanical horizons even further, enabling you to get a headstart on bulb growth or to keep bulbous flowers blooming a little longer.

Cut flowers do not, of course, last as long as potted or planted ones, but how beautifully they can grace a table. Many bulbs, once in bloom, make excellent, long-lasting cut flowers. These are attractive whether displayed alone or combined with foliage and other garden flowers. Even commercial cut flowers benefit by the addition of your own fresh-from-the-garden bouquets.

This chapter will tell you when to plant and when you can anticipate blooming for all the bulbs discussed in the Encyclopedia of Bulbs (page 82). The map below will help you identify your own particular growing zone. The list on page 53 will help you determine your local times of frost (a time when many bulbs need protection if left in the ground, or when they need to be dug up and stored through the winter).

You'll also discover various ways of bringing your garden indoors—whether as cut flowers (pages 54–55), as potted plants (page 55), as houseplants (page 55), as greenhouse plants (page 56), or as forced bulbs (pages 57–62). Your whole environment—indoors as well as outdoors—is a fitting home for the beautiful bulb.

Climate Zones

Locate your climate zone on this map (which is based on the USDA map of climate zones). Then examine the accompanying charts of planting dates and anticipated blooming seasons. They will help you determine what you can grow for a year of flowering bulbs.

Bear in mind that these zones are only approximate, based on average data, and that your local climate can be warmer or colder, especially in mountain regions. The map is intended as a guide to selecting bulbs that are successful for most people in the zone. If you live at a higher elevation than the average for your state, your climate may be one, two, or even three zones colder than the map shows. And if your garden is on a north-facing slope, it will be one zone colder.

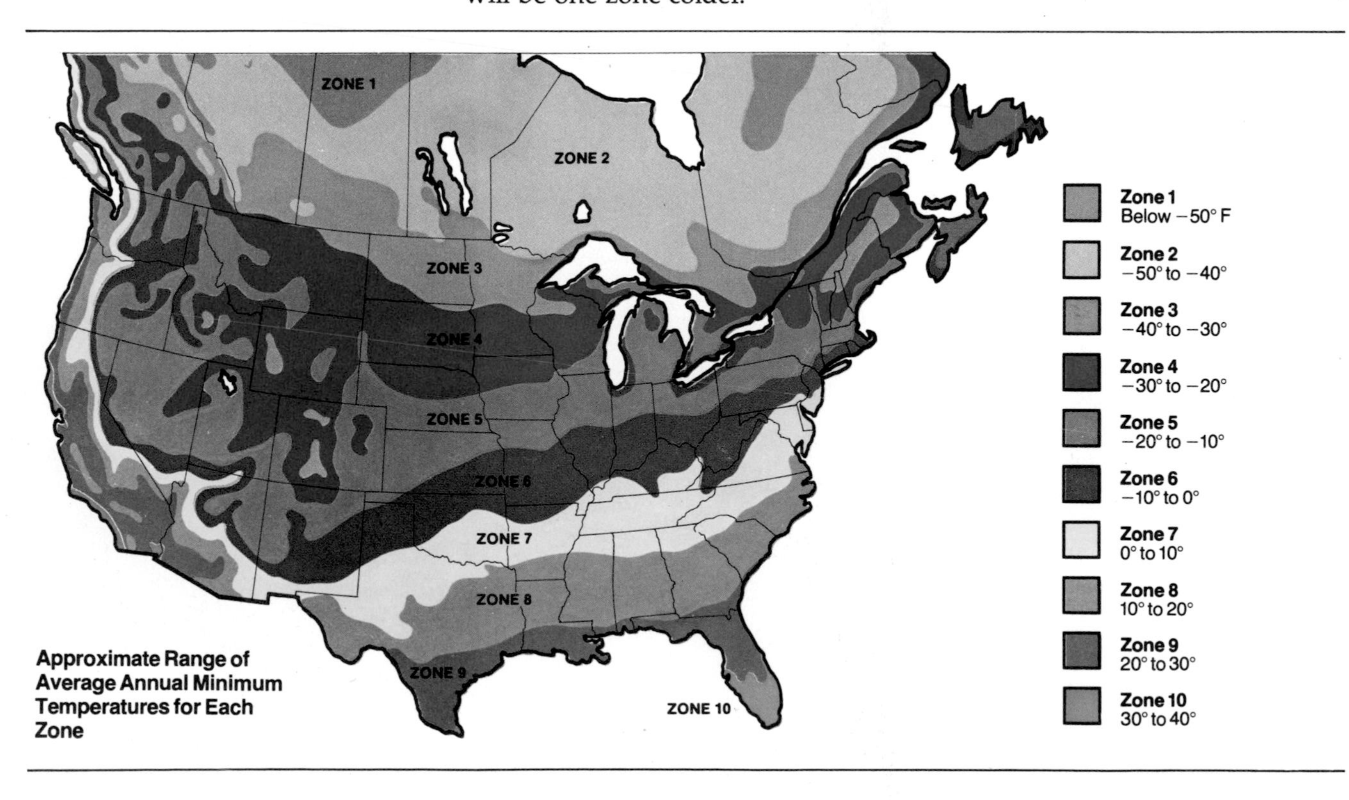

Approximate Range of Average Annual Minimum Temperatures for Each Zone

Bulb Blooming Dates

Zone	Early Spring	Spring	Summer	Late Summer and Fall	Winter
1	April 25– June 10	June 1– June 15	June 15– September 1	Usually not grown	Usually not grown
2	April 15– June 10	June 1– June 15	June 15– September 15	July 15– September 15	Usually not grown
3	April 1– June 1	June 1– June 15	June 15– September 15	July 15– September 15	Usually not grown
4	March 20– June 1	June 1– June 15	June 15– October 1	July 15– October 1	Usually not grown
5	March 15– May 15	Mary 15– June 15	June 15– October 1	July 1– October 1	Usually not grown
6	March 1– May 1	May 1– June 1	June 1– October 1	July 1– October 1	Usually not grown
7	March 1– May 1	May 1– June 1	June 1– October 15	June 15– October 15	Usually not grown
8	February 15– April 15	April 15– May 15	May 15– November 1	June 15 – November 1	November 1– February 15
9	January 1– Febuary 15	January 1– March 1	Bloom all year	June 1– November 15	November 15– Febuary 1
10	Usually not grown	January 1– April 1	Bloom all year	Bloom all year	Bloom all year

But even if the information in the charts seems to limit your selection, don't be discouraged from trying bulbs listed for a nearby zone. After all, half the fun of gardening is proving the experts wrong.

Anticipated Bulb-Blooming Periods

The chart of anticipated blooming seasons shows the gardening year divided into five seasons: early spring; spring; summer; late summer and fall; and winter. Locate the bulb you wish to grow and the season of its anticipated bloom. The climate zones indicate those areas in which the bulbs can normally be left in the ground all year, unless instructions for the bulb state otherwise. In other zones these bulbs will have to be planted and dug up each year.

Next, locate your zone on the chart of bulb-blooming dates and look across to the season to find the average dates when bulbs of that season bloom in your area. However, these dates are based on averages for the zone, so they will not necessarily hold true for your local area.

Local winter dates are determined by the first and last frost dates. After the anticipated blooming seasons chart, you will find U.S. cities and the average dates of their first and last frosts. Use these dates to determine when to mulch or otherwise protect your bulbs, or when to move them indoors. The first frost date also indicates the end of late-summer- and fall-blooming bulbs.

Planting dates indicate the best time for planting, and help you plan your own garden calendar. If your area has severe winters and the planting time is listed as fall or spring, spring is usually the better of the two.

Anticipated Blooming Seasons

Bulb	Early Spring	Spring	Summer	Late summer and fall	Winter	Outdoor hardiness zones	Planting times
Achimenes							
As houseplant or outdoors above 60°F.		●	●	●			Late winter or early spring
Agapanthus							
Evergreen species		●	●	●		9–10	Anytime
Deciduous			●			7–9	Anytime
As houseplant			●	●			Anytime
Allium		●	●			4–10	Fall
A. giganteum			●	●		6–10	Fall
Alstroemeria			●			8–10	Early spring or early fall
A. aurantiaca			●			6–10	Early spring or early fall
In protected containers			●			2–5	Early spring or early fall
Amaryllis belladonna				●		5–10	Late summer or early spring
Anemone							
Small daisy types	●	●				6–9	Fall
Large poppy types		●				9–10	Fall
Begonia							
B. grandis			●	●		6–10	Early spring; *B. tuberhybrida* must be dug in fall in all zones
B. tuber-hybrida		●	●	●		2–10	
Brodiaea		●	●			5–10	Fall; provide winter protection in Zones 5 and 6
Bulbocodium	●					3–10	Early fall
Caladium		●	●			8–10	Spring; dig up in fall in all zones
In protected pots		●	●			2–7	
Calochortus		●	●			5–10	Fall; provide winter protection in Zones 5 through 7
Camassia		●	●			3–10	Fall; dig up in fall in colder climates
Canna			●	●		7–10	Late spring or early summer; best to dig up in fall in all zones
In protected containers			●	●		2–6	
Chionodoxa	●					3–10	Fall
Clivia		●				9–10	Anytime
As houseplant		●					
Colchicum				●		4–10	Early fall
Convallaria		●				3–7	Fall or early spring
Forced, precooled	●	●	●	●	●		Anytime

Anticipated Blooming Seasons

Bulb	Early Spring	Spring	Summer	Late summer and fall	Winter	Outdoor hardiness zones	Planting times
Crocus	X				X	3–10	Early fall
Cyclamen							
Hardy species	X	X		X	X	5–9	Anytime
C. persicum							
As houseplant	X			X	X		Anytime
Dahlia			X	X		2–10	Spring; late summer in Zone 10
Eranthis	X					4–9	Early fall
Eremurus		X	X			5–9	Fall; provide winter protection in all zones
Erythronium		X				3–9	Fall
Eucharis							
As houseplant	X	X	X	X	X		Anytime
Freesia	X		X		X	9–10	
As houseplant	X		X		X		Fall; plant treated corms from the Netherlands in spring for summer blooms
Fritillaria		X				3–8	Early fall
Galanthus	X					3–9	Early fall
Gladiolus		X	X	X		5–10	Fall or spring; best dug up each year
Gloriosa			X	X		8–10	Anytime
As houseplant			X	X			Anytime
Hippeastrum	X				X	9–10	Fall to early spring
As houseplant	X				X		Fall to early spring
Hyacinthus	X	X			X	4–10	Fall
As houseplant	X	X			X		Fall
Hymenocallis		X				8–10	Spring or fall
Iris							
Bearded	X	X				5–10	Early fall
Bearded							
Dutch		X				7–10	Early fall
Reticulata	X					5–10	Early fall
Ixia		X	X			8–10	Fall
Ixiolirion		X	X			7–10	Fall
Leucojum							
L. aestivum	X				X	4–10	Fall
L. autumnale				X		5–10	Fall
L. vernum	X					4–8	Fall
Lilium			X	X		3–10	Fall or early spring
Lycoris				X		8–10	Midsummer
L. africana				X		9–10	Midsummer
L. squamigera				X		5–10	Midsummer

Anticipated Blooming Seasons

Bulb	Early Spring	Spring	Summer	Late summer and fall	Winter	Outdoor hardiness zones	Planting times
Moraea						8–10	Anytime
As houseplant							Anytime
Muscari						2–10	Early fall
Narcissus						4–10	Early fall
Tazetta types						8–10	Early fall
As houseplant							Anytime
Nerine						8–10	Summer to early fall
Ornithogalum						7–10	Fall
O. umbellatum						4–10	Fall
O. caudatum						8–10	Fall
O. nutans						5–10	Fall
Oxalis						9–10	Fall
O. adeno-phylla						6–10	Fall
O. bowiei						7–10	Fall
O. brasilensis						8–10	Fall
Polianthes						9–10	Spring: best to dig up in fall in all zones
Ranunculus						8–10	Fall or spring; best to dig up in fall in all zones
Scilla							
S. bifolia						4–10	Fall
S. peruviana						9–10	Early summer
S. siberica and ***tubergen-iana***						1–8	Fall
Sinningia							
As houseplant							Winter through spring
Sparaxis						9–10	Fall; best grown in containers
As houseplant							Fall
Sprekelia						8–10	Fall or spring
As houseplant							Fall or spring
Tigridia						7–10	Spring
Tritonia						7–10	Fall
Tulipa						3–7	Fall
Precooled bulbs for forcing						8–10	Fall
Watsonia						8–10	Late summer to early fall
Zantedeschia						8–10	Fall
As houseplant							Anytime
Zephyranthes						7–10	Fall

Average Frost Dates

	Last Frost	First Frost
Albany, NY	4/27	10/13
Albuquerque, NM	4/13	10/28
Altoona, PA	5/6	10/4
Asheville, NC	4/12	10/24
Atlanta, GA	3/21	11/18
Atlantic City, NJ	3/31	11/11
Augusta, GA	3/7	11/22
Bakersfield, CA	2/14	11/25
Baltimore, MD	3/28	11/17
Bangor, ME	5/1	10/4
Bend, OR	6/17	8/17
Berlin, NH	5/29	9/15
Binghamton, NY	5/4	10/6
Birmingham, AL	3/19	11/14
Bismark, ND	5/11	9/24
Boise, ID	4/29	10/17
Boston, MA	4/5	11/8
Bridgeport, CT	4/26	10/16
Buffalo, NY	4/30	10/25
Burlington, VT	5/8	10/3
Canton, NY	5/9	9/26
Caribou, ME	5/19	9/21
Centralia, WA	4/27	10/17
Charleston, SC	2/19	12/10
Charleston, WV	4/18	10/28
Charlottesville, VA	4/11	11/6
Cheyenne, WY	5/20	9/27
Chicago, IL	4/19	10/28
Cincinnati, OH	4/15	10/25
Cleveland, OH	4/21	11/2
Columbia, SC	3/14	11/21
Columbus, OH	4/17	10/30
Concord, NH	5/11	9/30
Corpus Christi, TX	1/26	12/27
Dallas, TX	3/18	11/17
Denver, CO	5/2	10/14
Des Moines, IA	4/24	10/16
Detroit, MI	4/21	10/20
Duluth, MN	5/22	9/24
El Paso, TX	3/26	11/14
Eugene, OR	4/13	11/4
Eureka, CA	1/24	12/25
Evansville, IN	4/2	11/4
Fort Smith, AR	3/21	11/10
Fort Wayne, IN	4/24	10/20
Fresno, CA	2/3	12/3
Grand Rapids, MI	4/25	10/27
Great Falls, MT	5/9	9/25
Green Bay, WI	5/6	10/13
Greenville, ME	5/27	9/20
Harrisburg, PA	4/9	10/30
Hartford, CT	4/22	10/19
Houston, TX	2/5	12/11
Huron, SD	5/4	9/30
Indianapolis, IN	4/17	10/27
Jacksonville, FL	2/6	12/16
Kansas City, MO	4/6	10/30
Knoxville, TN	3/31	11/6
La Crosse, WI	5/1	10/8
Las Vegas, NV	3/16	11/10
Lexington, KY	4/13	10/28
Little Rock, AR	3/17	11/13
Los Angeles, CA	—	—
Louisville, KY	4/1	11/7
Lubbock, TX	4/1	11/9
Marquette, MI	5/13	10/19
Marysville, CA	2/21	11/21
Memphis, TN	3/20	11/12
Miami, FL	—	—
Milwaukee, WI	4/20	10/25
Minneapolis/St. Paul, MN	4/30	10/13
Mobile, AL	2/17	12/12
Montgomery, AL	2/27	12/3
Nashville, TN	3/23	11/7
Newark, NJ	4/3	11/8
New Haven, CT	4/15	10/27
New Orleans, LA	2/13	12/9
New York, NY	4/7	11/12
Norfolk, VA	3/19	11/27
North Platte, NE	4/30	10/7
Ogden, UT	5/6	10/8
Oklahoma City, OK	3/28	11/7
Omaha, NE	4/14	10/20
Palm Springs, CA	1/18	12/18
Parkersburg, WV	4/16	10/21
Pasadena, CA	2/3	12/13
Peoria, IL	4/22	10/20
Philadelphia, PA	3/30	11/17
Phoenix, AZ	1/27	12/11
Pittsburgh, PA	4/20	10/23
Pittsfield, MA	5/12	9/27
Pocatello, ID	5/8	9/30
Portland, ME	4/29	10/15
Portland, OR	2/25	12/1
Providence, RI	4/13	10/27
Pueblo, CO	4/28	10/14
Raleigh, NC	3/24	11/16
Rapid City, SD	5/7	10/4
Red Bluff, CA	2/25	11/29
Reno, NV	5/14	10/2
Richmond, VA	4/2	11/8
Riverside, CA	3/6	11/26
Roanoke, VA	4/14	10/26
Sacramento, CA	1/24	12/10
St. Johnsbury, VT	5/22	9/23
St. Louis, MO	4/9	11/8
Salt Lake City, UT	4/13	10/22
San Diego, CA	—	—
San Francisco, CA	—	—
San Jose, CA	2/10	1/6
Santa Barbara, CA	1/22	12/19
Santa Fe, NM	4/24	10/19
Santa Rosa, CA	4/10	11/3
Savannah, GA	2/21	12/9
Scranton, PA	4/24	10/14
Seattle, WA	2/23	12/1
Shreveport, LA	3/1	11/27
Sioux City, IA	4/27	10/13
Sioux Falls, SD	5/5	10/3
Springfield, IL	4/8	10/30
Springfield, MO	4/12	10/30
Syracuse, NY	4/30	10/15
Tampa, FL	1/10	12/26
Texarkana, AR	3/21	11/9
Topeka, KS	4/9	10/26
Trenton, NJ	4/4	11/8
Tucson, AZ	3/16	11/19
Tulsa, OK	3/25	11/1
Washington, DC	4/10	10/28
Watertown, NY	5/7	10/4
Wichita, KS	4/5	11/1
Williamsport, PA	5/3	10/13
Wilmington, DE	4/19	10/26
Wilmington, NC	3/8	11/24
Winchester, VA	4/17	10/27
Worcester, MA	5/7	10/2
Yakima, WA	4/15	10/15

The flowers of *Iris reticulata* are a harbinger of spring in a northern garden.

An informal but carefully composed arrangement of flowering bulbs brings spring indoors.

Bringing the Garden Indoors

Flowering bulbs deserve to be seen close-up. The subtlety of individual forms, the complexity of their structures, their fragrances, their intense colors and delicate pastel hues are best appreciated at an intimate range. While bulbs are beautiful in the landscape, they seem to reach their pinnacle indoors as cut blooms, as container plants brought inside while flowering, or as houseplants.

Bulbs as cut flowers. Many bulbs make long-lasting cut flowers. Prolong the bouquet by selecting blooms that are just beginning to open, as well as a few buds that will open in a day or two. See the Encyclopedia of Bulbs, beginning on page 82, for special instructions on cutting different species. Cut the stems with sharp scissors or a knife. Leave as much foliage as possible on the plant to restore nutrients to the bulb. Carry a bucket of water along with you to the garden and immediately plunge the flower stems into the water after cutting. Don't, however, combine tulips and daffodils—the sap of daffodils injures the tulips. If you wish to combine them in an arrangement, first let each sit in its own container of water for a few hours.

Removing flowers causes the plant no harm; it may even make it stronger the following year, since the bulb will not have to exert energy in the maturing and seed-production stages of flowering. If you want cut flowers but don't want to take them from your landscape, consider planting a cutting garden of bulbs in an unobtrusive backyard area.

Commercial florists use the following trick to keep the stems of tall bulbs, such as tulips, straight. Lay a dozen or so flowers on three or four thicknesses of newspaper and wrap them up securely. Tie the bundle with a plastic-bag closure or string, and stand the package upright in deep water for a few hours or even overnight.

Tulips that are to be shipped by air are first wrapped in plastic film or newspaper and then refrigerated, flat on a shelf, for several days. When the flowers are ready to be used, they are given a fresh, sharp cut and plunged into just-warm water. If your garden contains many tulips at one time and you wish to store some for a while, you might try this idea.

Aspirins, sugar, or floral preservatives that keep other flowers fresh seem to do nothing for cut bulb flowers. However, a fresh daily cut, as well as clean, fresh water, will help prolong them. Don't push bulbs into florist's foam, especially hollow-stemmed flowers such as narcissus. It damages the end of the stem and reduces the flowers' life span. Although most bulbs enjoy deep water, narcissus seem to last longer in shallow water, just a few inches at the bottom of the container. However, they absorb a lot, so check on them daily to maintain the level.

When arranging bulb flowers, try to make them look as natural as possible. Don't constrict them into rigid lines or curves; position them so they can be appreciated for their natural grace, just as they grew in the garden. Because tulips, anemones, ornithogalums, and a few other bulbs will continue to grow even when in water, it is difficult to keep them positioned where you wish in bouquets. Some people use florist's wire under the heads and through the stem, but a more natural effect can be gained by simply turning them around or by recutting them when they go their own way.

Bulb flowers are beautiful displayed alone (all one kind or mixed), or combined with foliage and other garden flowers. Otherwise-dull flowers take on new dimensions when you add a few freshly cut bulb flowers.

Snip muscari and other tiny blooms to use for miniature arrangements for your bedside, the bathroom, a desktop, or individual dining-table bouquets for each person to enjoy. Combine them with tiny pieces of foliage or twigs of flowering fruit trees from the garden, if you wish.

Tuberous begonia blossoms are magnificent indoor decorations when floated in a shallow bowl.

Above left: Hyacinths that were brought into bloom outside are brought indoors for display.

Above: *Hippeastrum* makes a strikingly elegant houseplant.

Consider using clear glass containers to show off the succulent stems, since these contribute to the overall beauty of the flowers. Other good containers for bulb bouquets are baskets with metal or glass liners, pieces of Oriental porcelain, or terra-cotta pieces.

Bulbs as indoor gardens. Not only can you bring bulbs indoors as cut flowers, but you also can grow them in containers outdoors—where all their cultural requirements can be met—and then bring the pots indoors as they come into bloom.

When it's indoor-display time, clean up the containers and rest them on saucers of clear glass or plastic. Or hide the pot by placing it inside a decorative bowl, basket, or other holder. Be sure to provide an inside saucer or tray for drainage, since you'll need to continue watering the plants while they're indoors. If you'd rather not have the pot rim visible inside the decorative container, mulch with bark chips, green florist's moss, pea gravel, or other material. And when you do your fall or spring planting, consider planting bulbs directly into kitchenware or sturdy decorative containers. Any container can be used to grow bulbs if you drill a hole in the bottom for drainage.

The English have a knack for creating an indoor garden by combining several kinds of potted plants from the garden with ivy and other foliage in containers hidden inside large baskets. Or you can add blooming bulbs to your existing collection of houseplants to provide an island of spring, summer, or fall color in an otherwise green garden.

Many bulbs look exquisite when planted singly in pots appropriate to their size. Even one muscari or miniature narcissus in a tiny clay pot says just about all there is to say about gardening and spring. And a collection of individually potted hyacinths makes a wonderful tabletop decoration.

Bulbs as houseplants. While some bulbs can be grown indoors during certain seasons, others can be grown as year-round houseplants. These differ from "forced" bulbs. When you force bulbs, you create conditions necessary for the bulb to bloom out of season (see page 57); when you grow bulbs as houseplants you simply provide conditions similar to their native environment. (See page 68 for recommended soil mixtures for container-grown plants.)

Most bulbs grown as houseplants require at least 4 hours of direct sunlight each day and should be kept evenly moist during their growing and blooming period. During this time, feed them monthly with your favorite houseplant fertilizer. After blooming, most bulbs will begin to yellow and die back as dormancy sets in. When this happens, withhold water. Bulbs grown indoors usually prefer cool nighttime temperatures, so don't forget to turn down the thermostat.

Bulbs grown indoors are generally planted at the same time as those grown outside. The following paragraphs list the best candidates for blooming houseplants. Consult the Encyclopedia of Bulbs beginning on page 82 for descriptions of the plants and flowers, planting times, and cultural requirements.

Seasonal blooms. For spring-blooming bulbs, try *Ornithogalum* and *Sprekelia*, while *Ixia* and *Zephyranthes grandiflora* will bloom later in the spring and into early summer. For summer blossoms, plant colorful *Achimenes, Alstroemeria, Gloriosa,* or *Zephyranthes citrina*. *Zephyranthes candida* and *Nerine* will bloom from late summer into the fall, and florist's cyclamen (*Cyclamen persicum*) can provide you with long-lasting flowers from late in the fall to early spring. Other winter color can be provided by *Clivia* and sweet-smelling *Freesia*, which bloom into early spring.

Year-round blooms. Bulbs that bloom on and off all year, such as *Hippeastrum, Eucharis,* and *Oxalis*, do best if you force them into a period of summer dormancy by gradually withholding water until dormancy sets in. Common calla (*Zantedeschia aethiopica*) will also bloom best if given summer dormancy, but the small, colorful callas (*Zantedeschia rehmannii*), as well as *Sinninga* and *Moraea*, will bloom at any time of the year after a 3-month dormancy.

Bulbs for the Greenhouse

There are two ways to enjoy bulbs out of season: grow them in a greenhouse, or force them.

If you're lucky enough to own a greenhouse, consider adding some of the bulbs listed below to your plant collection. Your greenhouse—even if it's unheated—can be used to start bulbs early. This will give you larger plants to move outdoors when the weather permits. Tuberous begonias and dahlias often are started early this way.

At the other end of the season, the danger of frost in the fall can be your signal to bring any container-grown bulbs that are still in bloom into the protected environment of the greenhouse. There, you can enjoy them for a few more days or even weeks.

Here are some bulbs that frequently are grown in greenhouses. Some of them are too tender to grow outdoors except in the warmest climates. Others have such a spectacular appearance that they warrant the close-up attention reserved for greenhouse plants. Follow the cultural instructions given for each plant in the Encyclopedia of Bulbs starting on page 82.

But almost any bulb can be grown in a greenhouse if you give it the periods of cold that it needs to flower. To force bulbs, follow the directions on the next page.

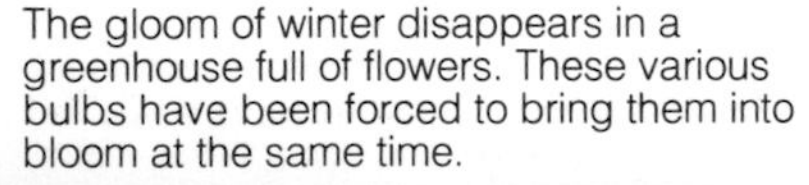
The gloom of winter disappears in a greenhouse full of flowers. These various bulbs have been forced to bring them into bloom at the same time.

Bulbs for Greenhouse Culture

Achimenes	*Hymenocallis*
Begonia	*Ixia*
Clivia	*Lillium*
Cyclamen	*Nerine*
Eucharis	*Oxalis*
Freesia	*Sparaxis*
Gladiolus (early-flowering small varieties and species)	*Tigridia*
Gloxinia	*Tritonia*
Hippeastrum	*Zantedeschia*

Forcing bulbs can extend the blooming season throughout the year.

Forcing Bulbs Indoors

Forcing a plant means making it bloom at a time or under conditions that are not natural. Hardy bulbs (see below) are particularly suited to this technique, and can provide a succession of indoor color from January to April.

Most gardeners force bulbs for displaying in pots, but if what you want is cut flowers in winter (which might be prohibitively expensive at the local florist), you can grow bulbs in flats. Forcing bulbs is easy enough; the challenge comes when you aim for a particular bloom date, such as Valentine's Day or Easter.

The most common hardy bulbs for forcing are daffodils, tulips, hyacinths, and crocuses. Others that can easily be forced include *Galanthus*, Dutch iris and *Iris reticulata*, grape hyacinths (*Muscari*), *Scilla tubergeniana*, *Eranthis*, *Ornithogalum*, and *Brodiaea*.

Allium, *Camassia*, *Scilla* species, and lilies are among the difficult-to-force bulbs, requiring special techniques and, usually, greenhouse conditions.

Forcing hardy bulbs involves four stages: (1) choosing the bulbs and, if necessary, preliminary storage; (2) planting; (3) cooling; and (4) forcing into bloom. Appropriate timing is the key to success for each stage.

Choosing bulbs for forcing. Whichever kind of bulb you choose, be sure the variety of bulb you purchase is clearly marked "good for forcing"—especially if, as is the case with tulips, hyacinths, and daffodils, a wide number of varieties is available. Some common varieties that are suitable for forcing are listed on page 60. Order your selections well in advance—in spring, if possible—to ensure their availability. Try to have them delivered no earlier than mid-September.

If you receive an early shipment, or if for some reason you can't plant the bulbs immediately, store them in a cool place (35° to 55°F.). A refrigerator is ideal. If the bulbs are packed in boxes or paper bags, open them up to provide ventilation. They can be stored this way for several weeks. But remember that bulbs are living plants: handle them carefully, and avoid exposing them to freezing temperatures.

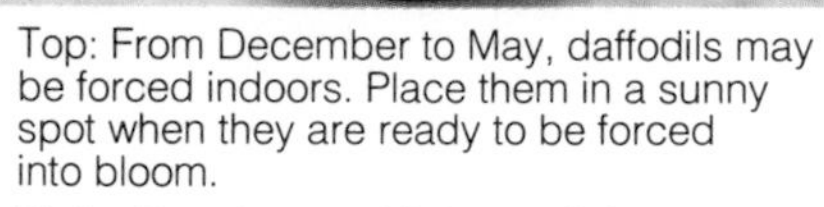

Top: From December to May, daffodils may be forced indoors. Place them in a sunny spot when they are ready to be forced into bloom.

Right: Supplemental light spotlights paper-white narcissus, allowing them to bloom in a shady spot indoors.

Above: Precooled bulbs for forcing, such as the hyacinth, can be bought at your garden center.

Arrangements such as this breakfast setting were planned months in advance. The bulbs may be forced in decorative containers that will match a particular setting.

Planting the bulbs. Bulbs that will bloom from January through April can be planted any time during October or November. The optimum cooling period is about 14 or 15 weeks. Even though you can cool them for anywhere from 13 to 18 weeks, the stem length will suffer, becoming short if the bulbs have been cooled for fewer than 14 weeks and long if the bulbs have been cooled for more than 15 weeks.

In general, plant around the beginning of October for January flowers, around the middle of October for February flowers, and in November for March and April flowers.

The planting medium will not only anchor the bulbs in place but also hold moisture for rooting. Since the bulbs already contain enough food for the developing flowers and roots, they don't need to be fertilized during the forcing process. Give them excellent, sharp drainage to keep them from rotting, but don't let them dry out. A good soil mix is 1 part loamy soil, 1 part peat, and 1 part sand. Use clean pots that have drainage holes in the bottom. If you use clay pots, soak them overnight so they won't draw moisture from the planting medium.

Fill each pot loosely with soil, just enough so that when the bulbs are placed in the pot, their tops are even with the rim. Don't compress the soil or press the bulbs into it: the soil under the bulbs should remain loose so roots can grow through it easily. After inserting the bulbs, fill the pots to the rim. The first watering will settle the soil enough to provide headspace for future watering. Water the pots 2 or 3 times to be sure that the soil is moist.

Plant about 3 hyacinths, 6 daffodils, 15 crocuses, or half a dozen tulips in a 6-inch pot or bulb pan. (When planting tulips, face the flat side of the bulb toward the outside of the pot. The first large leaf of each plant will then face outward, creating a uniform appearance.) Be sure to label each pot, noting the name of the variety, the planting date, and the date you intend to bring it indoors for forcing.

Bulb Varieties for Forcing

Type of Bulb	Time of Flowering	
	January and February	**March and April**
Tulipa	Red—'Bing Crosby', 'Olaf', 'Paul Richter' Yellow—'Bellona' White—'Hibernia' Pink—'Christmas Marvel' Variegated—'Kees Nelis'	Red—'Bing Crosby', 'Olaf' Yellow—'Bellona', 'Ornament' White—'Hibernia' Pink—'Peerless Pink' Variegated—'Golden Eddy','Edith Eddy'
Hyacinthus	Red—'Jan Bos' Pink—'Pink Pearl', 'Lady Derby' White—'L'Innocence', 'Colosseum' Blue—'Ostara', 'Delft Blue'	Red—none available Pink—'Pink Pearl', 'Marconi' White—'Carnegie' Blue—'Blue Jacket', 'Ostara'
Narcissus	Yellow—'Carlton', 'Unsurpassable', 'Dutch Master', 'Soleil d'Or' Bicolor—'Barrett Browning', 'Fortune', 'Ice Follies' White—'Mt. Hood', 'Paper-white', *N. tazetta* var. *orientalis*	Yellow—'Dutch Master', 'Soleil d'Or', 'Unsurpassable' Bicolor—'Barrett Browning', 'Magnet', 'Ice Follies' White—'Mt. Hood', 'Paper-white', *N. tazetta* var. *orientalis*
Crocus	Purple—'Remembrance' White—'Peter Pan' Striped—'Pickwick' Yellow—none available	Purple—'Remembrance' White—'Peter Pan' Striped—'Pickwick' Yellow—'Large Yellow'
Muscari (grape hyacinth)	Blue—'Early Giant'	Blue—'Early Giant'
Iris reticulata	Blue—'Harmony' Yellow—*I. danfordiae* Purple—'Hercules'	Blue—'Harmony' Yellow—none available Purple—'Hercules'

Adapted from Michigan State Extension Bulletin 593

Cooling the bulbs. All hardy bulbs need a period of cooling at temperatures between 35° and 50°F. to prepare them for later leaf and flower growth.

Some bulbs, especially tulips that are sold in mild-climate regions, have been "precooled" by the producer. These can be planted and forced immediately, or they can be treated as uncooled bulbs and cooled all over again. The second approach is best if you want your plants to bloom later in the season.

If you wish to recool precooled bulbs, or if you have held bulbs in the refrigerator for more than 3 weeks, subtract 3 weeks from the required cooling time.

During this deceptively "quiet" cooling period, all is not still—the plants' roots are forming. So keep pots moist. Since it's difficult to overwater when you have well-drained soil, check weekly to see if the pots need watering.

As to cooling methods, you can use any structure that will keep temperatures at 35° to 50°F. Many people find a root cellar or an unheated basement the most convenient; others prefer using an old refrigerator.

In Zone 6 and north, pots can be cooled in a coldframe or a trench in the garden. Either way, be sure to keep the pots from freezing. A coldframe used for this purpose should be well drained and in a shady location. After placing the pots in the coldframe, cover them with any loose insulating material: sand, sawdust, straw, or similar mulches.

To use the trench method, dig a trench about 6 inches wider than the pots, deep enough so that the pots are below the frost line, and long enough to hold all the pots you wish to cool. Spread an inch of gravel or cinders on the

Left: Daffodil shoots of this size are ready to be forced.

Above: Bulbs cooled in a cold frame are prepared for forcing.

bottom of the trench for drainage, and line the pots in the trench. Cover the pots with a few inches of sand, and finish by filling the trench with soil.

Just before freezing weather arrives, cover the trench with an insulating mulch—for example, bales of straw.

For a succession of blooms when using either of these methods, place pots in storage in the reverse order in which you will be removing them.

If you expect mice to make their home in the mulch and use your bulbs as food, top the trench with a ¼-inch-mesh wire screen before applying the mulch. To help you find what you want when you're ready to force each pot indoors, make a diagram of where the pots are placed in the trench and which bulbs are in each pot. If the weather is dry, water the pots frequently.

Forcing the blooms. At the forcing stage, the pots are brought out of their cooled environment into warmth and light, which trigger the formation of leaves and flowers. It takes about 3 or 4 weeks for bulbs that have been removed from storage to bloom. Bulbs planted on October 1 can be brought indoors around Christmas. Bring in a few pots every week after that for a continuous supply of blooms.

For best results, give the bulbs a temperature of 60°F. and direct sunlight. Rotate the pots regularly so that all the leaves receive an equal amount of light. To prolong the bloom, remove the flower buds from direct sunlight when they begin to color. Be sure to keep the soil evenly moist throughout the forcing period.

If you're aiming for a specific flowering date and you see that growth is

Right: Crocuses may be forced for out-of-season blooming.

Far right: Narcissus bulbs can only be forced once.

Top: Star-of-Bethlehem, or Arab's eye (*Ornithogalum arabicum*), can be forced.

Above: In addition to providing brilliant spots of color in a wide variety of deep colors, a few pots of hyacinths can perfume a whole room.

occurring too quickly, you can delay blooming by moving the pots to a cool (40° to 50°F.) room out of direct sunlight (not in darkness, however). When you want them to resume growing, gradually reaccustom them to sunlight.

Once hardy bulbs have bloomed, they cannot be forced again. A few, such as daffodils, can be transplanted into the garden in spring, but it will be 2 or 3 years before they reach their full blooming potential again. After forcing, most bulbs, such as tulips and hyacinths, are best discarded.

Soil-less forcing. Hyacinths sometimes are forced in special "hyacinth glasses." These are shaped like an hourglass, with an upper compartment for the bulb and a lower compartment into which the roots grow. Place the bottom of the bulb just above the water level in the lower section of the glass—the water shouldn't touch the bulb itself, or the bulb will rot. Add water as needed to maintain this level during growth. Cool the bulbs in their containers for 14 to 15 weeks; then place them where they will receive bright light and daytime temperatures of 60° to 65°F. Tiny bottles are sometimes available for growing crocuses the same way.

Planting bulbs in clear glass containers is an unusual method of forcing that lets you observe the mysteries of growth usually hidden beneath the soil. Children are particularly fascinated by this display of nature's activities.

Forcing without cooling. The 'Paper-white' narcissus (*Narcissus tazetta*), its yellow variety 'Soleil d'Or', and the Chinese sacred lily (*Narcissus tazetta* var. *orientalis*) can all be forced without cooling. Successive plantings made about 2 weeks apart, from mid-October on, can give you indoor blooms from Thanksgiving until late March.

The most common method is very easy. Using an undrained, decorative bowl, fill the container with enough pebbles, gravel, coarse sand, pearl chips, or similar material to reach to about 1 inch below the top. Add water until it's barely below the surface of the gravel. Set the bulbs on top; to hold them in place, add enough gravel to cover the bottom quarter of each bulb. Carefully maintain the water level.

An alternative method is to use vermiculite as a planting medium. Thoroughly saturate it, then squeeze out the excess moisture and place the vermiculite loosely in the container. Set the bulbs in place, and again partially cover them, leaving about three-quarters of each bulb visible. Keep the vermiculite evenly moist throughout the forcing process.

Tender narcissus are best kept in a cool (50° to 60°F.) spot in low light until they are well rooted and the shoots appear—usually about 2 to 3 weeks. Then bring them gradually into direct sunlight. Since these bulbs cannot be forced again after blooming, discard them.

Two spectacular South African bulbs which can be forced are *Babiania* (far left) and *Sparaxis*.

Bottom: Bulbs forced in a transparent container in a pebble medium have the added appeal of visible roots.

Careful soil preparation is important for bulb planting. Bulbs require good drainage to prevent rotting.

HEALTHY AND CARE-FREE BULBS

Bulbs require a minimum of care, but a knowledge of some basic facts and practices will help you keep them flourishing.

Bulbous plants are among the easiest plants to grow. They will bloom if you plant them in an average garden soil that has good drainage and if you water them throughout the growing season. You can even plant them in sand, pebbles, or marbles, as long as you give them a continuous supply of water. These marvelous little packages called bulbs contain enough nutrients to bloom without any further help from you.

However, if you want your bulbs to come back the following year, to remain in your garden for many years, or to naturalize and multiply themselves, they probably will need more care than just watering. Although bulbs thrive in many different types of soil, most need good drainage to keep from rotting. The easiest way to improve drainage is to add an organic amendment to the soil.

The bulb contains all the nutrients needed to make a flower the first year. After it has bloomed, however, it is exhausted and must replenish its nutrient supply in order to bloom again the following year. This replenishment takes place during the "quiet period" after the flowers have faded. During this period, the plant must be fertilized properly so that it will supply enough nutrients to make the next season's flowers.

Most bulbs are almost pest-free, but observing a few precautions will keep them healthy. If you know what problems to expect, you will be alert for potential trouble, and you can take corrective measures at the first sign of difficulty.

The basic elements of bulb care are simple and easy to apply. Observing these basics will ensure a profusion of flowers for your garden, your patio, and your home.

Selecting Healthy Bulbs

Success depends on the quality of bulbs. Always buy from a reliable source, whether you are shopping at local outlets or ordering from catalogs. As usual, you'll get what you pay for. It usually is more economical to buy fewer bulbs of higher quality from a good source than it is to search out bargains. Normally, larger bulbs mean more or larger flowers. The bulb suppliers on the list on page 141 offer catalogs from which you may order by mail.

When buying bulbs locally, be sure to examine them closely. They should be firm and free of deep blemishes, cuts, or soft spots. They should feel heavy for their size, not light or dried up like a seed. The basal plate must be solid and firm. However, small nicks and loose skins or tunics do not affect development. In fact, loose tunics help you spot harmful diseases.

Whether you purchase bulbs directly or by mail, plant them as soon as you get them. If this is not possible, store them in a cool place, such as a refrigerator. Do not store them in closed plastic bags—bulbs need to breathe. Instead, open the bags, or transfer the bulbs to paper bags.

Above: The apparent spontaneity of a spring bulb display is actually the result of careful planning and preparation.

Right: Tuberous begonias need shade. A site under a tree that casts light shade is ideal for them.

Choosing the Planting Site

Where you plant your bulbs has much to do with their success. First study the light requirements of the bulbs listed in the Encyclopedia on page 82; then read the instructions that come with the bulbs; and finally choose a spot in the garden that meets the specifications (even if it proves to be a container on the patio).

Most bulbs need bright sunlight, but a few actually enjoy shade. Spring bulbs that like bright sun, such as daffodils, do well underneath deciduous trees with high branches. These trees allow light to reach the bulb during the critical spring months.

Preparing the Soil

Bulbous plants adapt to many types of soil, but most prefer a loose, porous soil structure. With the exception of a few bulbs that tolerate swampy locations (for example Siberian iris), bulbs must have good drainage. If you cannot provide good drainage by adding soil amendments, preparing a raised bed, or installing a system to carry away excess water, you'll have to choose another site.

Before planting your bulbs, first prepare the soil so that the tender roots can easily move through the growing medium and so that water will drain through easily. Both heavy clay soils and extremely sandy soils can be improved by the addition of an organic amendment such as compost, humus, ground bark, sawdust, or peat moss. In heavier soils, organic material improves drainage and lets air move through the soil more readily. In sandy soils, organic matter holds moisture longer and keeps nutrients in the root zones.

Indeed, organic matter will improve just about any soil. To add the amendment, spread it over the surface of the planting area. Spread it at least 2 inches deep (but not more than 4 inches) and work it into the soil with a rototiller or spade.

Fertilizing

When you plant bulbs, mix some bone meal or superphosphate into the soil at the bottom of the planting hole. Phosphorus, the plant nutrient supplied by both these fertilizers, must be present deep in the soil, where the bulb roots are. And since it doesn't move readily through the soil, unlike other plant nutrients, it must be placed where the roots can reach it.

Fertilize the bulbs again when the foliage begins to emerge—usually in the spring. Spread a fertilizer containing nitrogen and potash (check the label to determine how much to use) on the ground around the plants and water it into the soil with a thorough irrigation. If the ground is exposed, stir the fertilizer into the top couple of inches before you water.

After this initial spring feeding, apply half the label amount of fertilizer every month until the foliage begins to yellow. If the bulb has evergreen foliage, continue the feeding program until fall; then stop; then begin again when growth resumes in spring.

Some bulbs, such as *Amaryllis belladonna* and *Colchicum*, bloom after the foliage has died. These plants should be fed only when the foliage is green. At this time they store all the nutrients they need to produce the flower.

Planting Suggestions

Consult the table on page 50 for appropriate planting times. As a rule, always plant bulbs as soon after receiving them as possible to prevent them from drying out. Lilies are especially delicate and should go into the ground immediately. If you live in a warm climate, delay planting early-spring bulbs until warm weather is past—keep them refrigerated or stored in a cool place.

The chart on page 68 gives recommended planting depths and spacings for the bulbs covered in this book. In general, plant most bulbs at a depth equal to three times their diameter at the widest point.

When planting a number of bulbs in one area, the easiest method is to dig up the area, set out the bulbs, and then cover them. But when planting smaller quantities, or when planting in crowded areas among other plants, it's best to dig each hole using a special bulb planter or a trowel. Position the bulb, cover with soil, and compact the soil with your hands.

Left: For massed displays of bulbs, excavate the entire bed. Note the addition of fertilizer.

Below: Use a special bulb planter when planting small numbers of bulbs or working in a crowded bed.

Planting Information

Bulb	Depth to Top of Bulb	Spacing Between Bulbs
Achimenes	½–1 inch	1 inch
Agapanthus	Just below surface	24 inches
Allium (large bulbs)	6 inches	12–18 inches
Allium (small bulbs)	4 inches	4–6 inches
Alstroemeria	6–9 inches	12 inches
Amaryllis	1–2 inches (Zones 9 and 10; 9 inches (other zones)	12 inches
Anemone (small types)	3–4 inches	2–3 inches
Anemone (large types)	3–4 inches	8 inches
Begonia grandis	1–2 inches	6 inches
B. × tuber-hybrida	½ inch	12–15 inches
Brodiaea	4 inches	3–5 inches
Bulbocodium	3 inches	4 inches
Caladium	1 inch	12–18 inches
Calochortus	2 inches	4–6 inches
Camassia	3–4 inches	3–6 inches
Canna	1–2 inches	15–18 inches
Chionodoxa	4 inches	1–3 inches
Clivia	Just below surface	18–24 inches
Colchicum	4 inches	6–9 inches
Convallaria	1 inch	4 inches
Crocus	4 inches	2–6 inches
Cyclamen (hardy)	2 inches	6–8 inches
C. persicum	Half of tuber above soil	12–18 inches
Dahlia	2 inches	15–30 inches
Eranthis	4 inches	3–4 inches
Eremurus	6 inches	18–36 inches
Erythronium	4 inches	4–6 inches
Eucharis	Tips at soil level	2 inches
Freesia	2 inches	2–4 inches
Fritillaria imperialis	6–8 inches	12 inches
Other species	4 inches	3–4 inches
Galanthus	4 inches	2–4 inches
Gladiolus	4–6 inches	4–6 inches
Gloriosa	4–5 inches	8–12 inches
Hippeastrum	Half of bulb exposed above ground	12–15 inches
Hyacinthus	6 inches	4–6 inches
Hymenocallis	3–5 inches	12–15 inches
Iris (bulbs)	4 inches	4–6 inches
Iris (rhizomes)	Just below surface	12 inches
Ixia	4 inches	3–6 inches
Ixiolirion	4 inches	3–4 inches
Leucojum	4 inches	4 inches
Lilium	4–6 inches	9–18 inches
L. candidum	1 inch	9–12 inches
Lycoris	3–5 inches	5–8 inches
Moraea	3–4 inches	12–24 inches
Muscari	2 inches	2–4 inches
Narcissus (large)	6 inches	6–8 inches
Narcissus (small)	4 inches	4–6 inches
Nerine	4–6 inches	6–8 inches
Ornithogalum (large)	6 inches	6–8 inches
Ornithogalum (small)	4 inches	3–4 inches
Oxalis	4 inches	4–6 inches
Polianthes	3 inches	6–8 inches
Ranunculus	1½ inches	3–4 inches
Scilla peruviana	5–6 inches	8–10 inches
Other species	4 inches	3–6 inches
Sinningia	1 inch	1 per 6-inch pot
Sparaxis	2 inches	2–3 inches
Sprekelia	3–4 inches	8 inches
Tigridia	4 inches	4–8 inches
Tritonia	3–4 inches	3 inches
Tulipa	6 inches	4–6 inches
Watsonia	4 inches	6 inches
Zantedeschia	3–4 inches	12–24 inches
Zephyranthes	1–2 inches	3 inches

Planting in Containers

Most bulbs to be planted in containers need a porous growing medium. Choose one that has equal parts of garden loam, coarse sand, and organic matter (such as peat moss or ground bark), or purchase one of the soil-less packaged mixes and add a little builder's sand or perlite to make it looser. Freesia, eucharis, ixia, moraea, and gloriosa require the addition of ground limestone at a rate of 3 to 5 ounces per bushel.

Shallow (4- to 5-inch deep) clay pots known as bulb pans are best for most bulbs. However, lilies, hippeastrum, and other large bulbs need regular pots (they don't fit in bulb pans). Shallow barrels, ceramic planters, plastic pots, and a host of other typical garden containers work satisfactorily.

Cover the drainage holes with pieces of broken crockery. Add the soil and position the bulbs in the pot, setting them closer than the planting spacing recommended on page 68. When grown in containers, bulbs in groupings should almost touch each other. Large bulbs such as lilies and hippeastrum are best planted individually in 6- to 8-inch pots. Plant tulips with the flat side facing the outside of the pot.

If the containers will be protected during winter, or if you're planting in spring after frost danger, set the bulbs so that their tips are just under the soil surface instead of at the depth suggested for garden planting. Fill the pot to the rim with loose soil. The first watering will settle the soil enough to make headspace for future waterings. Soak thoroughly after planting, and place the pots in a cool area until the bulbs root.

If the potted bulbs are to be forced, store or bury them as instructed on page 57. If they are to be grown as greenhouse specimens or houseplants, after they are rooted and shoots emerge place them where their light and heat requirements can be met.

If bulbs are to be grown outdoors in cold climates, plant them at the same time you would put out bulbs in the garden. Bulbs planted in fall should be protected in a coldframe or buried in a trench as for forcing, and should be left covered until frost danger is past. Bulbs planted in spring should be treated like bulbs planted in the ground.

In warm climates (Zones 8 to 10) you may need to use the trench method (see page 60) to provide the necessary cooling, as when forcing fall-planted bulbs. Place summer-blooming bulbs (those planted in the spring) where cultural conditions can be met.

Keep container-planted bulbs evenly moist throughout their growing and blooming period. Then, when the bulbs begin their rest period, reduce the watering.

Most container-grown bulbs should be repotted annually. Some, however, can remain in containers year after year—as long as winter protection is provided in cold climates. They can go indoors, be buried in the garden and mulched, or be stored in a basement or garage where they won't freeze. These include achimenes, agapanthus, canna, clivia, lilium, and zantedeschia. Each year at the normal planting time, knock out some of the soil and add fresh mixture.

Bulbs in Containers

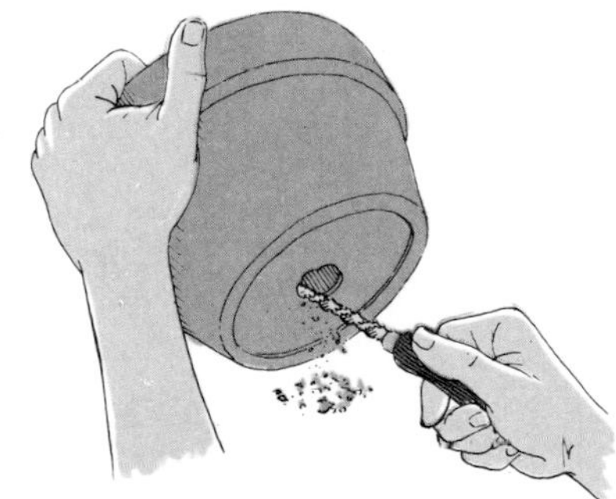

Check and enlarge drainage hole if necessary.

Fill the container with planter mix.

Plant the bulbs

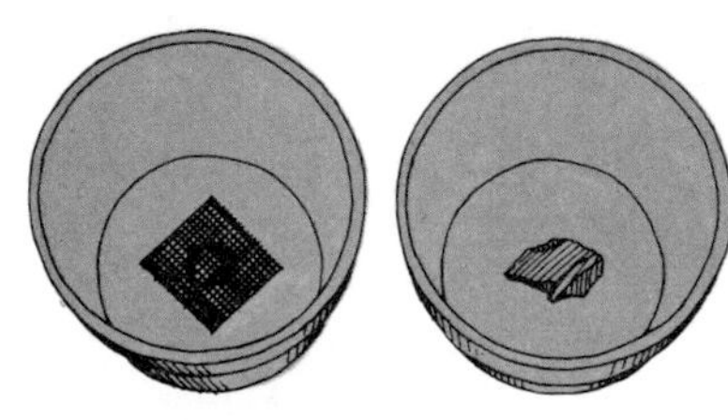

Cover drainage hole.

A mulch of shredded polystyrene may be used in cold climates.

A mulch simplifies maintenance by conserving water and preventing weed growth. The fir bark mulch shown here also acts as a background to show off yellow *Eranthis*.

Watering Bulbs

Water the planting area thoroughly after putting out bulbs, unless the ground is already soaked with rain (winter or spring rains usually provide all the moisture the bulbs need until they sprout). If you live in a dry climate the soil may tend to dry out, and you may need to provide additional water.

When the plants are a few inches tall, begin watering to keep them evenly moist throughout the growing and blooming period. Bulb roots grow deep, so water thoroughly; don't just sprinkle the surface. How much water to apply, of course, depends on the weather and the rate of growth. During active growth, bulbs need a lot of water. Continue to water after the blooms fade, until the foliage turns yellow.

Maintaining Planted Areas

There are many good reasons for mulching around bulb planting areas. A mulch keeps the garden neat, keeps soil from splashing onto foliage during watering or rains, reduces weeding, and visually enhances the area.

To keep bulb plants looking their best, remove spent flowers with scissors. This causes no harm to the bulbs and channels energy into storage of valuable nutrients instead of seed production.

However, leave the leaves—they must be allowed to remain, yellow, and ripen. Do not cut or pull them off unless you plan to discard the bulbs after they have bloomed. If you plant bulbs in a ground cover (for example, pachysandra or vinca) or in a perennial bed where flowering plants will distract attention from the fading foliage, you won't need to give the ripening foliage any special attention. But if the yellowing leaves offend you, they can be folded and tied to make a neater package in the garden.

Once the leaves have turned yellow, this means that the bulb has removed the nutrients and protein for use the following season. At this time, you can carefully pull or cut off the leaves.

Propagating Your Own Bulbs

Most gardeners know the arithmetic of basic gardening—that is, how to multiply by dividing. Most of the bulbs mentioned in this book can be multiplied (propagated) by dividing their tuberous roots, tubers, or rhizomes, or by separating new corms and bulbs from the original. In some cases—tulips, for instance—the old bulb disappears, leaving behind one or more offspring.

Methods of propagation

Scoring. This propagation method is commonly used on hyacinths, but also works on narcissus and scilla. Make three cuts through the basal plate. Store in a dry place for a few days until the cuts open. Dust the cut surfaces with captan, and place the bulbs in a warm, dark place with high humidity for a few months. After bulblets have formed, plant the mother bulb upside down in the garden. The bulblets will sprout in the spring.

Scaling. This method is used to propagate lilies or other scaly bulbs. Break or cut the scales close to the basal plate. You can remove the outer two rows of scales without damaging a large bulb. Dust the scales with captan and a rooting powder, then seal them in a plastic bag with damp vermiculite. Keep the bag at room temperature until bulblets form—about 2 months—then cool it in a refrigerator for another 2 months to overcome dormancy. The new bulblets can then be planted.

Bulb cuttings. Propagate narcissus, hippeastrums, and other tunicate bulbs by this method. Cut a mature bulb into eight sections vertically, then slip a knife between the scales and cut the basal plate so that there are four scale segments on each piece of basal plate. Plant these cuttings in vermiculite with the tips of the segments just above the surface. Treat the cuttings as in the directions for stem cuttings given on page 72. New bulblets will form between the scales in a few weeks.

Seeding. Almost all bulbous plants also can be propagated by the seeds that are produced when the flowers are allowed to develop fully. Usually, however, seedlings take several years to produce blooms. And since most bulbs are inexpensive, you'll probably choose to buy new ones when you want to add more flowers or plant a new area.

To start seeds outdoors, plant them about 4 times their own diameter below the surface. Keep the soil moist until the seeds germinate, then let it dry slightly between waterings.

To plant seeds indoors, plant them in damp vermiculite in pots or flats, just barely below the surface. If the seeds are very fine, don't cover them at all. Cover the flat or pot with plastic film and keep in a warm place. As soon as the seedlings are large enough to handle, transplant them to pots, using a mix like the one described on page 68.

Dividing rhizomes. Lift the rhizomes after flowering. Discard old rhizomes (without leaves) and cut the remainder into sections, leaving one fan of leaves on each section. Trim both the leaves and the roots to about 3 inches. Replant immediately just under the surface of the soil.

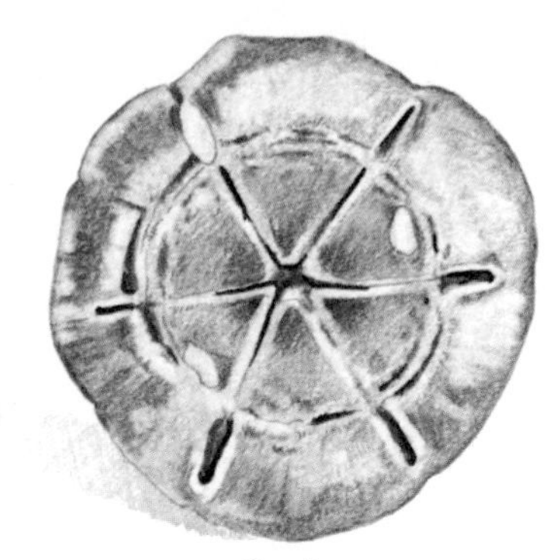

Scoring

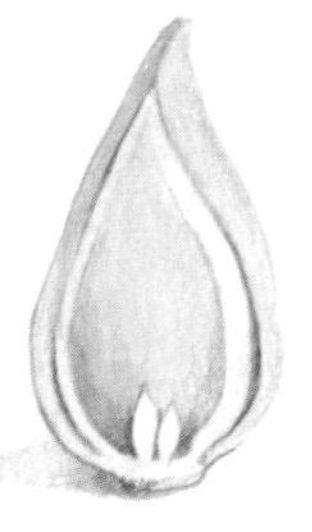

Scaling

Bulb cuttings

Methods of Propagation

Seeding

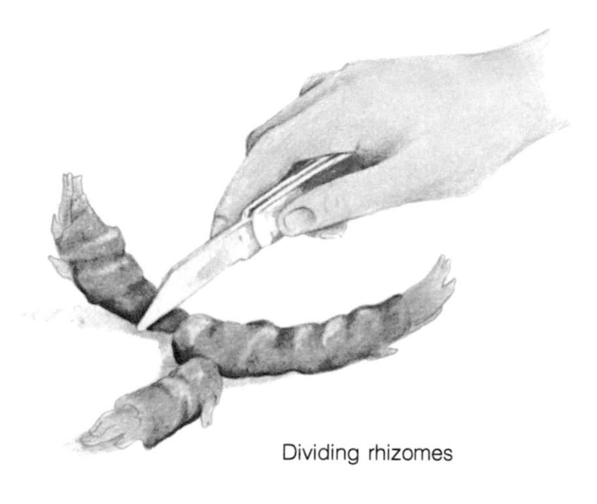

Dividing rhizomes

Stem cuttings. Cut any extra dahlia stems when they are about 4 inches high. Place the cutting in a pot of damp vermiculite and cover with a plastic bag, held away from the cutting with a loop of wire. Fasten the bag to the pot with a rubber band. Place the pot in a warm, bright spot, but not in direct sun. Water as necessary by placing the pot in a pan of water for ten minutes. Roots will form in a couple of weeks. Transplant to a soil mix when the root shows signs of new growth.

Dividing tuberous roots. After the eyes have begun to swell in the spring and are clearly visible, divide the tuberous root into segments. Each segment must have at least one eye. Dust the cut surface with captan and cure in a warm place for 2 days. Plant in the garden with the eyes about 2 inches deep.

Cormels. These tiny corms are formed around the edges of large corms. The shallower a corm is planted the more cormels it will form. Store cormels over the winter in slightly damp peat moss. Plant them in the spring, about 2 inches deep. A few might reach flowering size the first year, but most will need a second year of growth.

Bulblets and bulbils. Bulblet formation can be induced in some lily species. Disbud the mother plant and mound soil high around the stem, or bend the stem over and bury all except the top third in a shallow trench. Bulblets will form along the buried portion of the stem during the summer. Transplant them in the fall. Bulbils can be induced or enhanced in some species by disbudding the mother plant and, a week later, cutting off the top half of the stem.

You should plant both bulblets and bulbils about 2 inches deep in the fall before the first frost.

Methods of Propagation

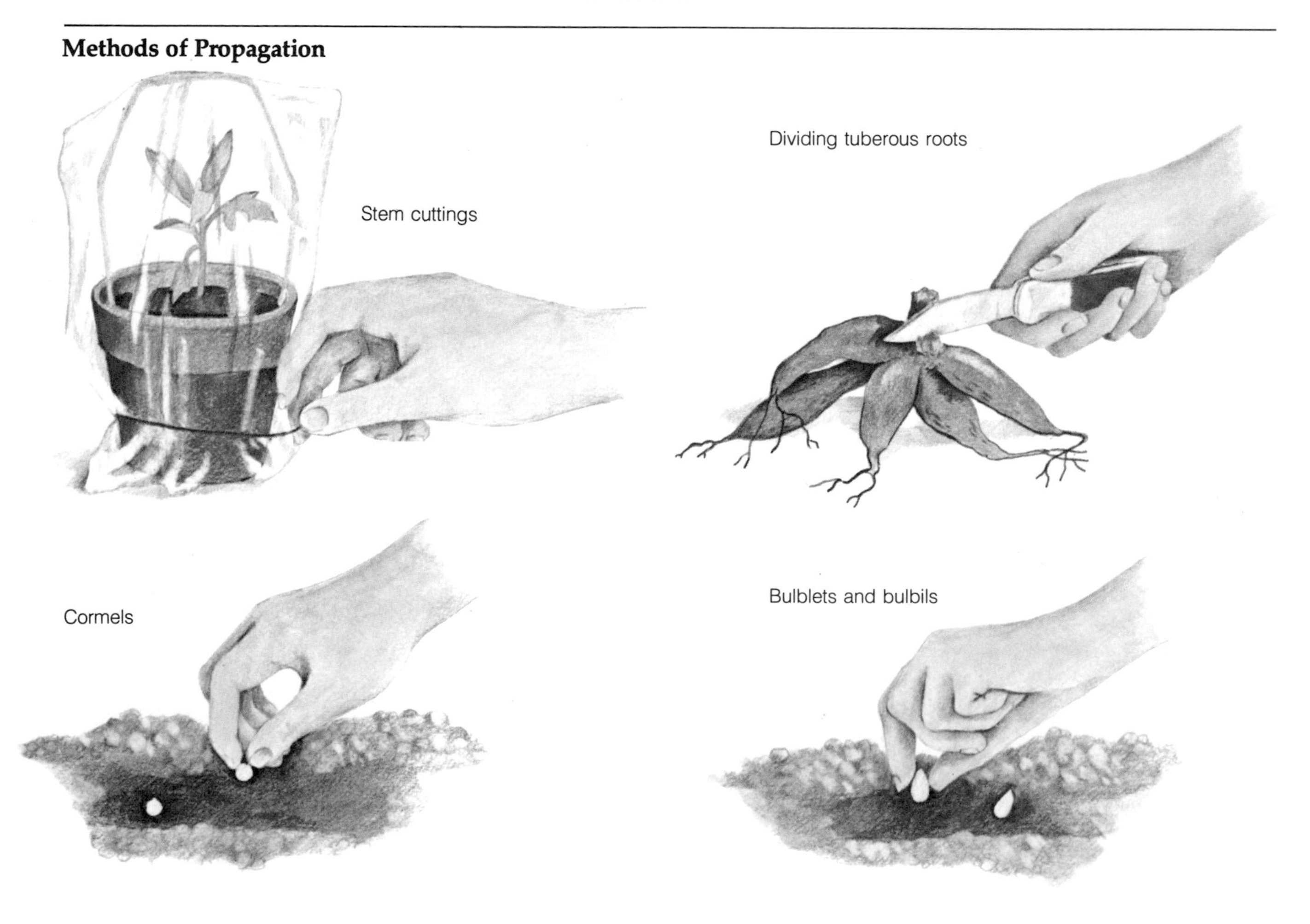

Propagation requirements. The following listing gives the best methods of propagating each of the bulbs described in the Encyclopedia of Bulbs (see page 82), plus the time and conditions necessary for seed germination.

Achimenes

Break off newly formed rhizomes during dormancy.

Separate rhizomes during growing season.

Root stem or leaf cuttings.

Seed germinates in 20 days at 70°F. Do not cover. Sow anytime.

Agapanthus

Divide rhizomes; evergreen types in the spring, deciduous types in the fall.

Seed germinates in 30 days at 65°F. Sow indoors in February or March.

Allium

Bulblets in early fall.

Bulbils that form on faded flowers.

Seed germinates in 10 to 30 days at 65°F. Sow indoors in winter or outdoors in spring.

Alstroemeria

Very difficult to propagate vegetatively.

Seed germinates in 20 days at 70°F. Start indoors in early spring.

Amaryllis

Bulblets in early spring or late summer.

Anemone

Divide tubers in late summer.

Arisaema

Divide offsets of tubers in the fall.

Easily grown from seeds planted directly in the garden.

Arisarum

Divide mat-forming rhizomes in the fall.

Begonia

Cut tuber into segments after the eyes begin to develop in early spring.

Stem cuttings in the spring.

Seed germinates in 30 days at 75°F. Seeds are tiny. Do not cover. Sow indoors in winter.

Brodiaea

Cormels in fall.

Bulbocodium

Cormels after foliage dies.

Caladium

Divide tubers during dormancy.

Calochortus

Bulblets after foliage dies.

Camassia

Bulblets in the fall.

Canna

Divide rhizomes in the spring.

Seed germinates in 20 days at 70°F. Soak overnight before sowing. Sow indoors in late winter or early spring.

Cardiocrinum

Plant offsets in the spring. Flowers will bloom in 3 to 4 years.

Plants will take 7 years to flower if grown from seed.

Chionodoxa

Divide bulbs in fall.

Sow seeds in the garden in late summer.

Top: Flaming red amaryllis plants form the focal point in a grouping of houseplants.

Above: *Allium* (flowering onion) planted in a bonsai container.

Left: Anemones add brilliant color to the garden and to cut bouquets.

Top: Colorful cyclamen attached to bark slabs can be moved easily.

Above: The violet petals and yellow pistil of this crocus can add intense color to a bulb bed.

Right: The collarette-form dahlia has an outer circle of petals surrounding an inner circle of shorter petals, often in different colors.

Clintonia
Divide rhizomes in spring.

By seed.

Clivia
Divide bulb in late spring.

Sow fresh seeds indoors. Germination takes a month at 75°F.

Colchicum
Cormels after foliage dies in summer.

Sow seed in the garden in late summer.

Convallaria
Divide pips in fall after foliage has died. Plant in fall or spring.

Crinum
Plant offsets in the fall. They are usually found below the bulb.

From seed, it will flower in 2 to 3 years.

Crocosmia
By division of corms.

By seeds planted just after ripening. Will self-sow readily in mild climates; propagate under glass in the north.

Crocus
Divide corms after foliage dies.

Sow seeds outside in late summer.

Cyclamen (florist's)
Cut old tubers into sections while dormant with at least one bud per section.

Seed germinates in 6 weeks at 65°F. Sow indoors in winter.

Cyclamen (hardy)
Divide tubers in the fall.

Dahlia
Divide tubers in the fall.

Stem cuttings in the spring.

Seed germinates in 7 days at 65°F. Sow indoors in early spring or outside in May.

Dierama
By division of corms. Will often bloom the first year and always the second.

Eranthis
Divide tubers in early fall. Plant immediately.

Seed takes 8 to 9 months to germinate. Will flower 4 years after seed is sown.

Eremurus
Divide tubers in late fall. Take care not to injure tender fleshy roots.

Sow seeds outdoors immediately after ripening. Germination is slow. Flowers in 5 years.

Erythronium
Remove and immediately plant offsets in summer. Will bloom in 2 to 3 years.

Eucharis
Offsets in early spring.

Freesia
Corms in mid-August through November.

Sow seed outdoors in fall after soaking for 24 hours.

Fritillaria
Offsets in late summer.

Sow seed outdoors in August as soon as it is ripe. Difficult to grow from seed.

Galanthus
Divide 4- to 5-year-old clumps after flowering and replant immediately.

Sow seed outdoors in June when harvested. Will bloom in 4 years.

Galtonia
Plant offsets taken from bulbs in the fall. Do not divide frequently; *Galtonia* performs best in thick clumps.

Easily grown from seed sown directly in the garden.

Gladiolus

Dig corms in late fall, and store until spring.

Separate cormels and plant in separate area in garden. Will grow to blooming size in 1 to 2 years.

Easily grown from seed, but hybrids may not stay true. Sow indoors in late spring. Will bloom in 2 years.

Gloriosa

Plant offsets or divide tuber in the spring.

Seed germinates in 30 days at 70° to 75°F.

Hippeastrum

Divide yearly, and plant offsets in fall.

Seed germinates indoors in 1 to 2 months at 70°F. Sow shallowly.

Hyacinthus

Bulblets produced by scooping or scoring the bulb.

Hymenocallis

Offsets planted in the fall.

Sow seed indoors in winter.

Hypoxis

Seeds planted in the garden is the easiest method of progagation.

Divide short rhizomes in the fall.

Iris (bulbous)

Divide bulbs every 5 years and plant offsets in October.

Sow seeds outdoors in fall.

Iris (rhizomatous)

Divide every 4 years. Each rhizome section should contain at least one node. Plant July through September.

Sow seeds outdoors in fall.

Ixia

Remove offsets in summer, after foliage dies back.

Ixiolirion

Remove offsets from bulbs after flowering in the spring. Will bloom in 4 years.

Leucojum

Lift and divide clumps in early summer (after flowering) and replant immediately.

Seed is slow to germinate. Sow outdoors in September. Will flower in 4 to 5 years.

Lilium

Lift and divide clumps in autumn. Take extra care not to bruise or break scales. Plant immediately.

Bulbils on leaf axils may be detached in early autumn and planted. Remove first and second years' flowers to ensure strong bulb development.

Sow late-summer-flowering lilies in spring and early-flowering varieties in late summer.

Scales can be rooted.

Lycoris

Separate offsets from parent plant in August and set in ground. Will bloom in 4 years.

Moraea

Separate and replant corms in September.

Sow outdoors in autumn or spring, according to particular species. Will bloom in 4 to 5 years.

Muscari

Offsets are prolific and can be detached from 4-year-old bulbs that are *carefully* lifted for division.

Sow seed outdoors in April. Blooms will appear in 4 to 5 years.

The regal, magnificent lily adds beauty to a garden. Plant different lilies for a succession of blooms from spring well into fall.

Flower colors of the tall iris are accentuated against its own foliage.

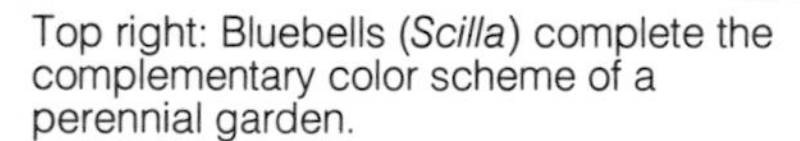

Top right: Bluebells (*Scilla*) complete the complementary color scheme of a perennial garden.

Top left: *Ornithogalum* can be grown from seed or offsets.

Bottom: Gloxinias (*Sinningia speciosa*) can be grown indoors or in pots on a shaded terrace or porch.

Narcissus

Offsets may be divided from parent plant every 2 to 3 years in July. Plant in the early fall. Blooms appear in 3 to 4 years.

Nerine

Offsets form freely, so 3- to 4-year-old plants become too crowded. Dig, divide, and replant bulblets in the spring or autumn.

Seed germinates quickly. Sow in spring as soon as it loosens from the flower head. Seedlings pull under the surface as they grow. Will bloom in 3 to 4 years.

Ornithogalum

Plant offsets in autumn. Will bloom in 3 years.

Sow seed outdoors in spring. Will bloom in 3 years.

Oxalis

Plant offsets or root divisions in late August to September. Will bloom in spring.

Sow seeds outdoors in late August to September.

Polianthes

Divide tubers from parent plant after flowering, and store until spring.

Puschkinia

Gather offsets and plant early in the fall.

Ranunculus

Offsets form around older tuberous roots. Set out in October or November.

Sow seeds outdoors in April. Will bloom the following year.

Scilla

Lift and divide clumps every 4 years. If bulblets are small, divide several to a clump.

Seed sown in spring will bloom in 5 years.

Sinningia

Plant tubers in spring.

Cut large tubers into segments with at least one bud per segment.

Stem or leaf cuttings with a small piece of stalk attached will form a tuber and bloom by the second year.

Offshoots with 3 or 4 leaves form on stem of mature plant and can be planted to bloom sooner than other cuttings.

Seed germinates indoors in 2 to 3 weeks at 70°F. Do not cover seed. Seed sown in winter will bloom the first season.

Sparaxis

Offset from base of corm can be planted in September.

Seed germinates easily. Sow outdoors in autumn. Corms form readily and flowers begin in 2 to 3 years.

Sprekelia

Plant offsets in early September in moderate climates and in April in colder areas.

Sternbergia

Divide bulbs in August or September, only when crowded.

Tigridia

Planted in spring.

Seeds sown outdoors in May flower in 3 to 4 years and are true to color.

Tritonia

Large corms form at base of parent. Plant in October.

Rhizomes produce corms at nodes. If of adequate size, they can be removed and planted in the fall. Will bloom in 2 years.

Seed sown outdoors in autumn germinates in 4 to 6 weeks. Plants will die back but should not be disturbed. Will bloom in 3 to 4 years.

Tulipa

Detach offsets when bulb is lifted after flowering. Remove any first-year blooms to strengthen bulb.

Vallota

Gather offsets after blooming and plant in 6-inch pots with a light, well-drained soil. Will bloom well only if roots are very crowded, so do this infrequently. Repot to a slightly larger pot only when crowded, taking care to disturb the roots as little as possible.

Veltheima

By seed.

Watsonia

Remove and plant cormels after flowering. Will bloom in 2 years.

Seed germinates in 1 month. Sow in spring. Will bloom in 3 to 4 years.

Zantedeschia

Divide tubers in fall. Leave 2 to 3 shoots on each division.

Seed germinates in a month at 75°F. Sow indoors in early spring. Do not cover seed. Will bloom in third year.

Zephyranthes

Remove offsets after flowering, when plants are dormant. Replant immediately.

Sow seed outdoors in spring.

Zigadenus

By division in the fall.

By seed.

Left: Tall calla lillies (*Zantedeschia aethiopica*) add a regal touch to a garden.

Bottom: Tulips offer the gardener an extraordinary range of colors.

After flowers fade, put bulb containers in an out-of-the-way place so the bulbs can continue to grow and store up energy for the next season. Leave the foliage attached; here it is tied for the sake of neatness.

Harvesting and Storing

Dig carefully when uprooting bulbs to make room for other plants, or when digging those that are not hardy in your climate and that must be stored for the winter. Likewise, be careful when planting in an area containing bulbs. The spading fork is the best digging tool; it is least likely to slice through a bulb. Discard any bulbs that have been badly wounded.

After digging bulbs, shake off loose soil and dry the bulbs for about a week in a shady, protected spot with good ventilation. Then brush off any remaining soil, and dust with a fungicide to help control rot and other diseases.

Store the bulbs in a porous bag or a shallow tray filled with dry peat moss, perlite, vermiculite, or sand. This keeps them from drying out, but still allows them to breathe. Store them in a cool (35° to 50°F.), dry place where they will not freeze.

Controlling Pests and Diseases

Most of the pests and diseases that attack bulbs appear in the chart on the next three pages. Check with your county extension agent or local garden center for information about other problems and effective controls. When using garden chemicals, be sure to follow the label instructions.

Preventive care is the best way to deal with pests and diseases. The Brooklyn Botanical Garden recommends the following precautions.

- ☐ Keep planted areas clean. Weeds and rubbish make good hiding places for insects and fungus spores.
- ☐ Disinfect storage areas (cellars, flats, and so forth) with a fungicide that won't injure plants. Ceresan and zineb are good for this purpose.
- ☐ To reduce damage from insects and diseases, dust all stored bulbs with an insecticide powder in combination with a fungicide. Such dusts are available at seed stores and garden centers.
- ☐ Spray growing plants regularly to protect them against both diseases and insects.
- ☐ Dig up and discard all plants with mosaic or yellows diseases, *Botrytis*, or scab.

Aphids

Common hosts: Anemone, Begonia, Dahlia, Gladiolus, Hyacinthus, Iris, Lilium, and *Tulipa.*

Damage: Curled or twisted leaves, yellowing of foliage, spread of virus disease, honeydew secretion attracts ants.

Control: Spray with malathion, diazinon, Sevin, or Orthene. Wash off with garden hose.

Botrytis

Common hosts: Begonia × tuberhybrida, Dahlia, Gladiolus, Hyacinthus, Lilium, Narcissus, and *Tulipa.*

Damage: Spotted, then blighted leaves and flowers; slimy, collapsed leaves or flowers; gray, fuzzy mold on plant.

Control: Apply garden fungicide to soil and bulbs before planting. Pick up old leaves and flowers. Plant bulbs in areas with good area circulation. Discard diseased bulbs, flowers, and foliage.

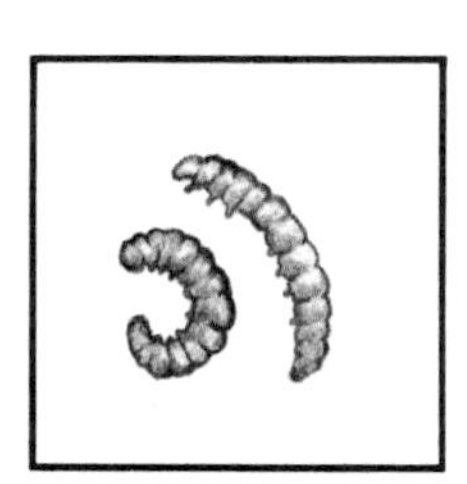

Cutworm, spotted

Common host: Amaryllis.

Damage: Torn and eaten flower petals.

Control: Spray with Sevin.

Fungus diseases

Common hosts: Most bulbs.

Damage: Stunted yellow growth; mushy or dried-out bulbs.

Control: Discard rotted bulbs. Dip bulbs in captan or Phaltan fungicide before planting or storing. Handle bulbs carefully when planting or digging to avoid damaging surface.

Gophers and other ground-dwelling animals

Common hosts: Tulipa, Crocus, and many others.

Damage: Eaten bulbs.

Control: Plant in raised beds or containers. Set traps. Use poisoned bait. (Check with local authorities regarding any restrictions.) Plant in underground "baskets" made of 1-inch or smaller wire mesh.

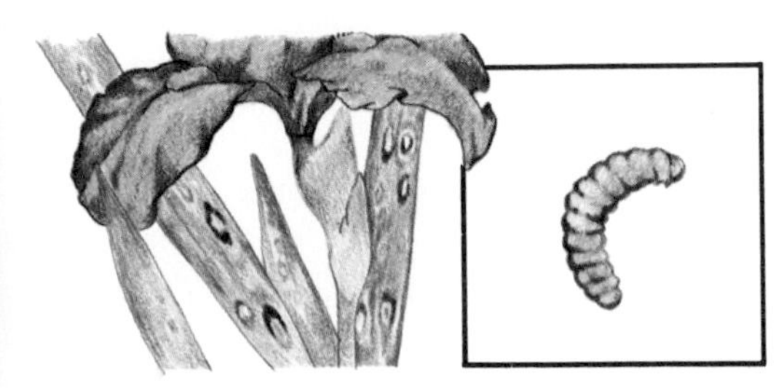

Iris borer

Common host: Iris.

Damage: Tunnel through leaves; bore into rhizomes, causing rot.

Control: Spray with malathion weekly during April and May.

Japanese beetles

Common hosts: Canna and *Dahlia*.

Damage: Chewed holes in stems, leaves, or flowers.

Control: Spray with malathion, Sevin, or diazinon. Set beetle traps. Remove by hand.

Mites

Common hosts: Amaryllis, Begonia, Crocus, Cyclamen, Freesia, Gladiolus, Hyacinthus, Lilium, Narcissus, and *Tulipa*.

Damage: Speckled leaves; lack of growth.

Control: Spray plants with malathion or diazinon. Destroy badly infested bulbs.

Mosaic or yellows diseases

Common hosts: Canna, Crocus, Dahlia, Gladiolus, Hyacinthus, Iris, Lilium, Narcissus, Scilla, and *Zantedeschia*.

Damage: Mottled or yellow leaves; distorted foliage or flowers; stunted growth.

Control: Destroy infected plants. Destroy disease-spreading aphids. (See page 78.)

Narcissus fly larvae

Common hosts: Amaryllis, Galanthus, Hymenocallis, Leucojum, Narcissus, and *Zephyranthes*.

Damage: Eaten bulb centers; yellow, deformed leaves; stunted growth.

Control: Discard soft bulbs. Dust soil or bulbs with diazinon. Sprinkle soil around plants with naphthalene.

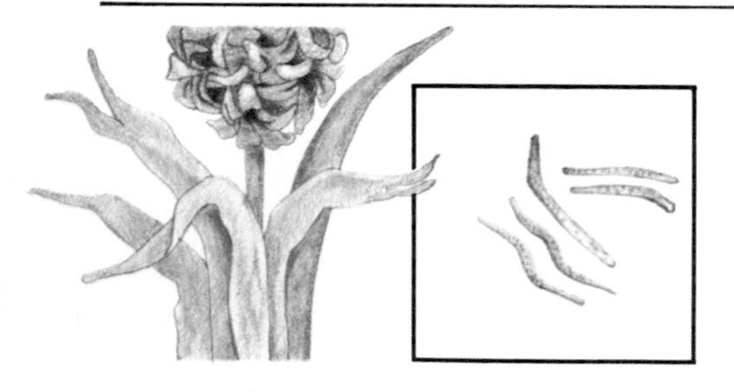

Nematodes

Common hosts: Dahlia, Galanthus, Gladiolus, Hyacinthus, Iris, Lilium, Lycoris, Narcissus, and *Tigridia*.

Damage: Deformed or split leaves; yellow and brown blotches on foliage; browned bulb tissue.

Control: Destroy infested plants and bulbs. Fumigate soil. (Consult your local nursery or garden center.)

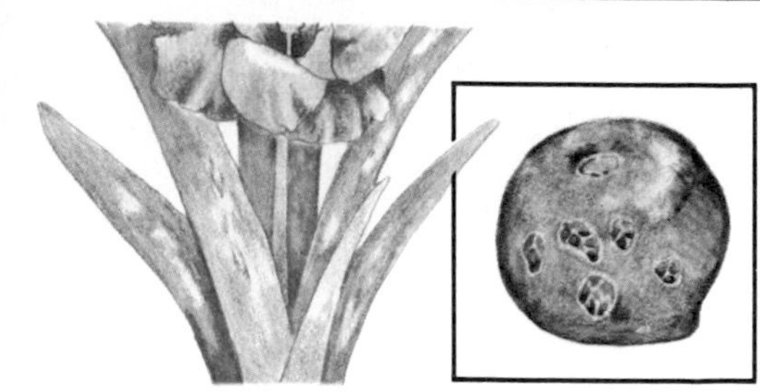

Scab

Common host: Gladiolus.

Damage: Lesions on corms; spotted leaves.

Control: Dust corms with fungicide. Discard infested corms.

Slugs and snails

Common hosts: Agapanthus, Canna, Dahlia, Lilium, and *Tulipa*.

Damage: Holes in leaves; eaten young shoots; slime trails.

Control: Put out snail bait when first shoots emerge.

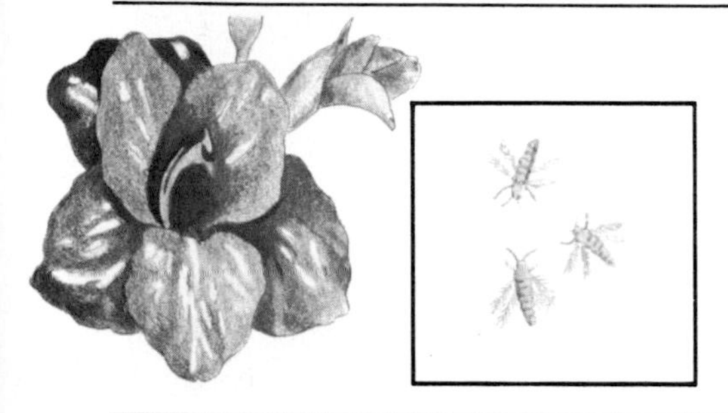

Thrips

Common hosts: Allium, Amaryllis, Begonia, Dahlia, Freesia, Gladiolus, Lilium, and *Sinningia*.

Damage: Streaks of gray or brown on foliage or flowers; sticky brown surface on stored bulbs.

Control: Spray growing plants with malathion or Orthene. (Check labels.) Dust bulbs with diazinon before storing.

Wireworms

Common hosts: Begonia, Dahlia, and *Gladiolus*.

Damage: Eat their way through stems causing plants to collapse.

Control: Treat bulbs and soil with diazinon before planting.

For form and color, *Zantedeschia elliottiana* (golden calla lily) is difficult to surpass.

ENCYCLOPEDIA OF BULBS

The wide range of bulbs now available makes it certain that you can find the right bulbs to suit your needs and growing conditions.

It's one thing to admire a colorful display of bulbs in a public garden or a longtime-gardener's backyard, but it's quite another to decide which to plant in your own soil. Which will survive best under your climatic conditions? Which demand slavish care, and which virtually take care of themselves? Which offer blazing jungle colors, which muted, subtle shades? Which will scent the air around them with lush, opulent fragrances? And—most important of all—which will please you?

If you turn to the following pages, you will find descriptions and cultural guidelines for those bulbs that do best in home gardens. Included are those that are most popular, also some that you may not yet be familiar with.

The bulbs are listed alphabetically by their botanical names (genera). Under each botanical listing you will find the bulb's common name(s). In many cases, the bulb's place of origin is mentioned. This will give you a clue about the conditions it naturally favors. The lengthy descriptions of each bulb will give you an idea of the appearance and growth habits of various species of each genus. If a bulb does well as a house plant or greenhouse specimen, or has other special uses (such as for cut flowers), that too is mentioned.

Bulbs for Specific Purposes

If you are looking for a bulb to fill a special need in your landscape, consider the following.

Bulbs for fragrance: *Convallaria, Cyclamen purpurascens, Freesia, Gladiolus tristis, Hyacinthus, Hymenocallis, Ixiolirion, Lilium, Lycoris squamigera, Muscari, Narcissus* (selected), *Polianthes, Puschkinia,* and *Tulipa sylvestris.*

Bulbs as carpeting: *Anemone blanda* and varieties, *Chionodoxa, Crocus, Eranthis, Galanthus, Muscari, Ornithogalum umbellatum,* and *Scilla.*

Bulbs for moist (not wet) areas: *Camassia, Convallaria, Erythronium, Muscari armeniacum, Ornithogalum umbellatum,* and *Trillium.*

Bulbs for dry areas: *Allium, Calochortus, Crocus, Eremurus, Iris reticulata* and varieties, *Narcissus* species, *Ornithogalum umbellatum, Oxalis, Sternbergia,* and *Tulipa* species.

Bulbs for partial shade: *Achimenes, Allium moly, Anemone, Arisaema, Begonia grandis, B. × tuberhybrida, Caladium, Camassia, Chionodoxa, Colchicum, Convallaria, Crocus, Cyclamen, Eranthis, Erythronium, Fritillaria, Galanthus, Lilium* (selected), *Muscari armeniacum, Narcissus* (selected), *Ornithogalum nutans, O. umbellatum, Scilla, Trillium,* and *Tulipa sylvestris.*

Bulbs for accent: *Canna, Dahlia, Eremurus, Fritillaria imperialis, Gladiolus, Hyacinthus orientalis, Hymenocallis, Lilium, Lycoris squamigera, Narcissus, Polianthes tuberosa,* and *Tulipa.*

Bulbs for rock gardens: *Allium, Brodiaea, Bulbocodium vernum, Calochortus, Chionodoxa, Crocus, Eranthis, Fritillaria, Galanthus, Hypoxis, Iris danfordiae, I. reticulata, Leucojum, Lilium, Muscari, Narcissus* species, *Ornithogalum umbellatum, Oxalis adenophylla, Puschkinia, Scilla, Sternbergia,* and *Tulipa* species.

In the quest for bulbs that best suit your own needs, you may find it helpful to use this directory in several different ways. First, skim through: note those plants that appeal to you (glancing at the photos will help clarify this point) and write down their names on a piece of paper.

Then read about those plants in more detail, bearing the following questions in mind:

Will it fill my needs? In other words, will the plant fill the role you intend for it? Consider color, size, shape, texture, and bloom date (see pages 50–52 for planting and flowering seasons).

Will it please me? This question may seem obvious, but many gardeners get so overwhelmed by the cultural instructions demanded of them and by the opinions (both solicited and unsolicited) offered by other people that they forget that the whole point of planting bulbs is to experience the pleasure of seeing and living with them.

Not that you can disregard cultural information, of course. The directory gives sunlight requirements and anything unique to that bulb. Otherwise, follow the general information under "Healthy and Care-Free Bulbs" on pages 64–81. For planting depths and spacing, see page 68. For methods of propagation, see page 71. For a list of mail-order bulb suppliers, see page 141. And if you wish to learn much more about any of the bulbs described here, contact one of the plant societies listed on page 141.

Achimenes (Magic Flowers, Nut Orchid, Widow's-Tears)

These colorful plants—often called magic flowers and sometimes called widow's-tears or nut orchids—bear long-lasting flowers, which come in yellow, pink, blue, purple, or white, and cover the plants from early spring through fall.

Achimenes generally are grown as houseplants, greenhouse plants, or outdoor container plants in areas where temperatures do not drop significantly at night. They are tender, thin-stemmed plants that prefer partial shade. When displayed in hanging planters, they don't need staking. Otherwise they do.

In late winter or early spring, plant the scaly rhizomes in a porous soil

Achimenes Andersonii'

mix. Keep evenly moist and feed about once a month with any liquid houseplant fertilizer.

When the flowers fade, gradually withhold moisture and let the plants become dormant. The rhizomes can be stored in their pots in a cool (45° to 60°F.), dry place. Then, at the beginning of the next growing season, remove most of the soil, add a fresh mixture, and begin normal culture. Or, if space is a problem, unpot the rhizomes and store them for the winter in perlite, dry peat, or vermiculite, and keep them protected from the cold.

Agapanthus orientalis

Agapanthus (African Lily, Lily-of-the-Nile)

Although known commonly as lily-of-the-Nile, *Agapanthus orientalis* (sometimes listed as *A. africanus* or *A. umbellatus*) actually came from the South African mountains: thus its other name, African lily. This summer-blooming plant and its hybrids are evergreen, with strap-shaped leaves and tall (to 3 feet) stems topped with a cluster of trumpet-shaped flowers in blue, purple, or white. Agapanthus has long been a favorite in outdoor gardens of the West and other mild climates. In colder zones it often is grown as a houseplant or in containers so it can be given winter protection.

Look also for a white *Agapanthus* cultivar and a dwarf: *A.* 'Rancho Dwarf', with white flower stalks up to 2 feet, and *A.* 'Peter Pan', with lots of deep blue flowers on 12- to 18-inch stems.

All cultivars provide superb cut flowers that stand out dramatically when mixed in summer bouquets. Cut them as the first buds begin to open.

Plant *Agapanthus* in rich soil—in light shade in hot climates or in full sun in cooler areas. Whether you grow the rhizomes in the ground or in containers, allow the roots to become crowded to produce more flowers. Divide the plants every 5 years, or when flowering declines. Fertilize monthly during their active growing season and give them plenty of moisture. In cold climates, provide protection before the first frost.

Allium giganteum

Allium (Onion and Garlic)

These decorative relatives of edible onions and garlic offer a wide variety of blossom sizes, shapes, and colors. They are also one of the longest-blooming groups of bulbs in the garden. The foliage grows directly from the ground, and graceful, leafless stems topped with flowers in rounded clusters rise from its midst.

A number of species are cultivated by commercial cut-flower growers, both because they are attractive and because the blooms remain fresh for a long while in a vase. And fortunately (except when the foliage is cut or

Allium neopolitanum

bruised), most of the decorative alliums do not smell like their edible bulb relatives.

The most spectacular allium is *A. giganteum,* with 5-foot flower stalks topped by huge round balls of lilac-colored flowers in summer.

Allium christophii (once known as *A. albopilosum*), or stars of Persia, grows up to about 3 feet, and has early-summer lilac flower clusters that are about the size of dinner plates. The interesting strap-shaped leaves with fuzzy white undersides reach 1½ feet in length.

Blue allium, *A. caeruleum* (also sold as *A. azureum*), produces blue flowers on 12-inch stems in summer.

The late spring blooming *A. karataviense* has lovely silvery pink flower clusters about 4 inches in diameter atop 8-inch stalks.

Golden garlic, *A. moly* and *A. flavum,* produces bright yellow flower clusters 2 to 3 inches wide on stems 12 to 18 inches tall in midsummer.

One of the most popular alliums (the species is grown commercially) is the late-spring-flowering *A. neapolitanum* and its improved cultivars. These produce clusters of sweet-smelling white flowers on 12-inch stems.

For shady areas, *A. triquetrum* provides a touch of white that enlivens other late spring and early summer blooms. Bell-like, rose-striped flowers cluster above its ground-hugging foliage.

Most alliums require full sun, rich soil, and excellent drainage. Begin fertilizing when plants first emerge, and apply plenty of moisture during the growing season. Plant alliums in the fall. If you leave the bulbs in the ground for several years, they will fill your planting area with bloom. Apply winter mulch in cold zones.

Alstroemeria (Peruvian Lily)

While Peruvian lilies are not true lilies, they do come from the Andes, in South America. They make splendid additions to the bulb garden, especially because of their beautiful, extremely long-lasting cut flowers.

Growing to heights of 4 feet, these statuesque plants display their large, clustered blossoms from early summer through July. Colors vary with species: *A. aurantiaca,* growing 2½ to 4 feet high, produces orange blooms with red stripes, and its cultivar 'Lutea' comes in bright yellow. *A. ligtu* hybrids appear in several pastel combinations.

Tuberous roots are fragile and difficult to divide, but winter-sown seed will produce plants that bloom the first year. These natives of the Southern Hemisphere like plenty of sun, except where summer temperatures are very high. Plant or transplant container-grown plants from the nursery at any time.

Like most bulbous plants, alstroemerias require excellent drainage. The

Alstroemeria aurantiaca

tall stems are rather delicate, and must be staked if you have much wind. Alstroemerias make excellent, long-lasting cut flowers.

A. aurantiaca survives even cold climates north of its normal limit of hardiness (Zone 6), if it is well protected by mulch or planted in a sheltered, sunny area. Grow the plants in containers if you have any doubt about their ability to survive outdoors in winter. Store the containers where they will remain cool but be protected from freezing. In the South, bulbs can be left in the ground all year.

Amaryllis belladonna

Amaryllis (Amaryllis, Belladonna Lily, Naked Lady)

A number of bulbous plants—especially the container plant *Hippeastrum* and many of the *Lycoris* species—are commonly called amaryllises, because they are look-alike members of the same family. But the only true *Amaryllis* species in the bulb garden is *A. belladonna,* the fragrant belladonna lily (sometimes sold as *Brunsvigia rosea* or *Callicore rosea*).

In fall and winter in warm climates, or in early spring in cold climates, the first phase of growth begins. The foliage appears and lasts through summer, when it finally withers. In early autumn, leafless brown stalks are topped with trumpet-shaped blossoms, giving the plant its other intriguing common name, naked lady.

Plant the bulbs in full sunlight during early spring or late summer. When the foliage appears, feed the bulbs with any complete fertilizer. Water freely while the foliage is growing, and also later, while they are in bloom. In warm regions the bulbs are almost indestructible, and they last quite well as far north as Zone 5 when protected.

Naked ladies grow well in pots and should be planted in late summer. When the foliage is growing, feed these potted plants with any liquid houseplant fertilizer. Keep the pots indoors in winter to let the foliage mature. Leave the bulbs in pots year-round; they do not like being disturbed, and they flower best when crowded.

Anemone (Lily-of-the-Field, Magic Flower, Windflower)

Two types of brightly colored anemones are welcome additions to spring gardens: small, daisylike flowers are originally from European mountain slopes and woodlands; large, poppylike anemones are native to southern Europe and are very popular florist flowers.

The hardy, daisy-type species include *A. apennina,* commonly called Apennine anemone, and the Greek anemone, *A. blanda*. Both species come in blue, pink, rose, and white. *A. apennina* grows on 6- to 9-inch stems. The Greek anemone is slightly shorter, but its colors are more intense.

The poppy anemone, *A. coronaria,* produces large white, red, blue,

Below: *Anemone blanda*

Below left: *Anemone coronaria* de Caen strain

indigo, or violet flowers. The deep blue-black stamens are striking. Popular strains include the French anemone (the de Caen strain) which produces single flowers, and the St. Brigid and St. Bavo strains, which are semi-doubles in the same mixed anemone colors. St. Bavo adds soft pastels of the hues and sports brightly contrasting centers.

Poppy anemones are popular in bouquets. Cut them when the petals are unfolding but the center is still tight.

All anemones require fast-draining soil. *A. apennina* enjoys partial shade; all others need full sun. Plant all anemones in the fall in warm climates. North of Zone 7, plant in early spring and dig up for storage in late summer. All anemone tubers sprout best when soaked in tepid water for a day before planting. The tubers of poppy-flowered anemones look like claws: plant them claw-side down. Stems can be lengthened by applying nitrogen fertilizer when buds appear.

Arisaema (Jack-in-the-Pulpit)

Called "Jack-in-the-pulpit" because of its curious spathe-and-spadix flower, *Arisaema triphyllum* is an easily grown woodland plant with attractive, bold foliage all season long, and brilliant red-orange berries in late summer and fall. And the flower, while curious, is also quite handsome. The green or whitish poker-shaped spathe is hooded over by a greenish or brownish striped spadix. The three-lobed leaves gradually enlarge over the season to as much as 20 inches across. The entire plant can stand as high as 30 inches by the end of the season.

Arisaema sikokianum

Arisarum proboscideum

While easily started from seed, germination is slow, usually taking two seasons. More commonly *Arisaema* is planted as a corm. Small ones (¾ inch in diameter or less) are best planted 2 to 4 inches deep, while the larger ones should be planted 5 to 8 inches deep. Although adaptable to most woodland soils (high in organic matter), a moist soil, slightly on the acid side is best. In good situations they will self-sow readily. Give them partial to dense shade. *Arisaema* are excellent for the natural woodland or shady garden. They also perform beautifully in pots.

Arisaema sikokianum is a recently-introduced Japanese species. A striking plant with almost sinister beauty, the leaves are boldly variegated with cream, and the large, club-shaped spadix, which is a brilliant white, contrasts with a dark, blackish hood richly veined with cream and brown.

Arisarum (Mouse Plant)

Arisarum proboscideum is an interesting, rather than showy plant, named for its odd flowers. An Arum, like *Arisaema*, the flower has a rod-shaped spadix almost completely hooded by a blackish-maroon spathe, which has a whitish base and an extremely long, whip-like apex, looking for all the world like a mouse's tail. The flowers are often hidden by the foliage, and one has to hunt to find them. Sometimes they are held more or less vertically just above the foliage, resembling a mouse diving for cover.

Native to Italian woods, this is an easy plant to grow, but may be difficult to find in commerce. It is useful for the dense, lush mats of foliage it provides as the bulbs multiply with age. The rich green leaves are spade-shaped and attractive all season long. Give it a semi-shady spot with slightly acid soil high in organic matter. The mousey blooms appear in April or May.

Begonias (Tuberous)

Begonias provide some of the brightest colors for shady spots in the garden. This large genus includes a wide variety of plants. Many of them, such as the fibrous-rooted begonias, rex begonias, and most of the species begonias grown by specialists are not discussed here. But the tuberous begonias that belong in a book on bulbs are the most spectacular plants in the genus.

Tuberous begonias produce flowers 2 to 10 inches in diameter in a variety of forms and colors ranging from vivid reds, fluorescent oranges, and bright yellows to pastel apricots, pinks, and pure white. Many are variegated, edged or shaded with other colors. The form varies from upright plants that reach 12 to 18 inches in height through the Multiflora varieties that grow

Begonia × tuberhybrida

into bushy plants with small flowers, to the Pendula, or hanging basket varieties with stems that trail to 18 inches.

Tuberous begonias are generally divided into two main sections: winter-flowering tuberous begonias, including Cheimantha begonias and Hiemalis or Elatior begonias, and summer-flowering tuberous begonias, including Tuberhybrida begonias, Multiflora begonias, and Pendula begonias.

Winter-flowering tuberous begonias. These are largely florist plants, limited to indoor or (preferably) greenhouse growing, and consequently somewhat more difficult to maintain than the summer-flowering types. Often smaller that the summer-flowering begonias, they are very showy, with many smallish flowers nearly covering the large, round, bright green leaves. Cheimantha begonias are sometimes called Christmas begonias due to the time of year when they are usually sold as florist plants. Bushy plants, the flowers come in pink or white shades and are single. These are the easiest of the winter-flowering begonias to grow in the home, and their flowers last longer than the Hiemalis begonias described below. Cheimantha begonias need cool temperatures (70°F. days, 60°F. nights) and humid air with ample circulation but free of frequent drafts of outdoor air. Keep the soil constantly moist but never soggy. Give them bright, indirect light with a couple of hours of direct light each day, but avoid placing them next to a very sunny window or the foliage will burn.

Hiemalis or Elatior begonias are winter-flowering types that are more difficult to grow in the home than the Cheimantha begonias, but are showier. The showy flowers can be double or single, in many shades of pink, red, white, salmon and apricot. They appreciate cooler temperatures than the Cheimanthas (55°–60°F. days), and will not tolerate water on their leaves, being more susceptible to mildew and rot. Water them from below. Otherwise, their culture is the same as for the Cheimantha begonias.

Above: Begonia × tuberhybrida
Left: Begonia × tuberhybrida, Multiflora Group

Summer-flowering tuberous begonias. These are divided into three main types: Tuberhybrida, and its two subdivisions, Multiflora and Pendula.

Tuberhybrida begonias have been bred extensively over the years, resulting in many forms and colors. The newer varieties have flowers up to 8 or 10 inches across and good strong stems to support them, nearly perfect color and form, and greatly improved disease resistance. The tuberhybridas are especially useful massed in beds, or grown in pots for the patio, terrace, or porch. They are excellent as a cut flower for corsages or to float in a bowl. They are grouped according to their flower form:

1. *Camelliaeflora* (camellia type) varieties have incredibly large, fully-double flowers up to 10 inches in diameter.
2. *Ruffled camellia* varieties are similar to the above with petals that are swirled, frilled, fluted, or ruffled on the edge.
3. *Fimbriata* (carnation-flowered) varieties have double flowers, the petals of which have saw-tooth edges.

4. *Cristata* (crested) varieties have single flowers with four petals, each of which has a tufted crest resembling a cockscomb.
5. *Crispa marginata* (single-frilled crispa) varieties have huge, single flowers with crispy-frilled petal margins.
6. *Narcissiflora* (daffodil-type) varieties are interesting, more for the collector than for show. The fragrant flowers vaguely resemble giant daffodils.
7. *Marginata* varieties are of two types, double and single. Both have petals edged with a thin line of a contrasting color.
8. *Marmorata* varieties have bicolor flowers of the camellia type. Most are slightly smaller, with flowers in the rose shades, streaked with white.
9. *Picotee* varieties are similar to the Marginata types in that the edges are lined with a contrasting color. But the line is not precise, irregularly bleeding and blending softly into the main shade. It is found in both the camellia and rose forms.
10. *Rosebud* varieties should not be confused with the rose form. In the rosebud varieties, the central petals form a cone similar to a rosebud.
11. *Rose form* varieties look like roses, but are actually a camellia type that has been developed further.
12. *Single-flower form* varieties are beautiful in their simplicity, but not too widely grown.

Multiflora begonias are quite different from other tuberhybridas, bearing much smaller flowers, but making up in quantity what they lack in size. The long-lasting blooms nearly cover completely the foliage on compact, 12- to 18-inch plants. They are easier to grow than the other tuberhybridas, taking more sun and less moisture, and seldom need pinching or staking. Give them light, well-drained soil that is rich in organic matter.

A cross between the Multiflora and the camellia-flowered Tuberhybrida has resulted in the Grandiflora begonias. Closely resembling the multifloras, they have larger flowers, that are more reliably double, and every bit as profuse.

The Pendula begonias, or hanging-basket begonias, are the most difficult of the summer-flowering tuberous begonias to grow. They are sensitive to excessive wind and sun and to moisture in both air and soil. They should have warmth and humidity, and require heavy feeding frequently.

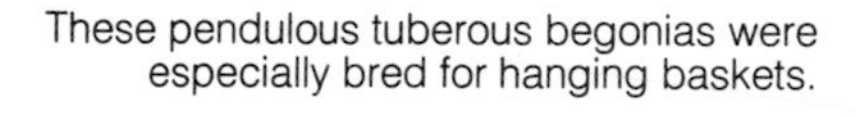

These pendulous tuberous begonias were especially bred for hanging baskets.

Begonia 'Saturn' (left) and 'Snowbird' (right)

Most pendulas have smallish double flowers of the camellia type. Some are picotees, and some are single. Most trail up to 18 inches, and have been bred for hanging baskets. In order to encourage the trailing habit, pinch out the crown shoots, or allow the plants to wilt slightly in dry soil. The best specimens, like all tuberous begonias, are grown from the largest tubers.

Cultivation of summer-flowering tuberous begonias. The summer-flowering tuberous begonias are all grown as summer annuals, either in containers or outdoors in the ground. They are best planted in light shade, and should not be stuck away in some dark, shady place in the garden. Give them well-drained soil rich in organic matter, and feed them about twice a month with liquid fertilizer.

Remember that when planting tubers, the larger the tuber, the larger the plant will be and the more flowers it will have. For pots, tubers should measure at least 1 ½ inches across. Small, one-inch tubers are fine for mass planting outdoors in beds. For exhibition, tubers should measure 3 inches.

Tuberous begonias should be planted when pink buds, or eyes, appear on the tuberous roots in the early spring. Where the climate is cold, begin the roots indoors 7 or 8 weeks before you anticipate the last frost and warming temperatures. Start them in 3-inch deep flats or trays filled with moistened peat moss; press the root, concave side up, into the growing medium until the top is flush with the medium. Transfer to 6- or 8-inch pots of half potting soil, half peat moss when the plants are about 4 inches high. Keep them evenly moist until after the last frost, at which time they can be transferred outdoors in larger pots or planted directly in the garden.

Summer-flowering tuberous begonias should be dug up in the fall after the first light frosts have turned the foliage brown. Pot-grown plants should be removed from the soil at this time, also. Clean the tubers of soil and let them dry in a dark, well-ventilated place. Do not remove the stems and foliage from the tubers forcefully; allow them to dry and fall off. Store the tubers in a root cellar or similar cool, dark, dry place until spring.

Begonia grandis (Begonia evansiana) is known as the hardy begonia. It blooms through summer until frost, with small pink flowers on plants that grow to about 24 inches high. It is an excellent choice for the shady garden, particularly for its lush, exotic-looking foliage. It is hardy over winter outdoors as far north as protected areas of Zone 5. Plant it in the early spring in rich, well-drained soil high in organic matter. It can be easily propagated from the tiny bulblets that appear at the joints of the leaf stems. In fact, it will tend to spread quite rapidly by itself in this manner.

Brodiaea hyacinthina

Brodiaea (Firecracker Flower, Grass Nut, Ithuriel's Spear, Pretty-face, Wild Hyacinth)

Excellent as cut flowers or naturalized in the landscape, *Broadiaea* species produce grassy foliage and clusters of small (½- to 1¾-inch) flowers on stems from 1 to 3 feet fall.

In order of blooming, species to consider are: Early spring brings *B. pulchella* (known also as *B. Capitata* or *Dichelostemma pulchellum*), the wild hyacinth or blue-dicks, which has blue to violet flowers. It is followed shortly by *B. ixioides* (*B. lutea* or *Triteleia ixiodes*)—commonly known as pretty-face or golden brodiaea because of its bright yellow blossoms—and by *B. laxa* (*Triteleia laxa*), known as grass nut or Ithuriel's spear, with violet to purple, sometimes white, flowers.

Late spring through midsummer offers *B. elegans* and *B. coronaria* (*B. grandiflora*), the harvest brodiaeas, with violet to purple flowers. It also brings *B. ida-maia* (sometimes sold as *Brevoortia ida-maia* or *Dichelostemma ida-maia*), called the firecracker flower because of its bright red flowers tipped with green.

Early summer-blooming white *B. hyacinthina* (also called *Triteleia hyacinthina*) has clustered purple-tinged flowers.

Brodiaeas are native to the American West, and they need bright sun and dry summers—or in areas with rainy summers, excellent drainage. They need abundant moisture while they are actively growing, but after blooming they must dry off. Plant corms in the fall. In Zones 5 and 6 they'll require winter mulching. North of Zone 5, brodiaeas should be planted in containers so they can be protected from the cold.

Bulbocodium vernum

Bulbocodium (Spring Meadow Saffron)

A good companion to spring crocuses in warm climates, *Bulbocodium vernum*, the spring meadow saffron, signals the arrival of the new year with bright pink or lavender-pink flowers. Narrow, short-lived leaves do not appear until the plant is in full bloom. This European member of the lily family makes a colorful addition to the rock garden, where other green plants can make up for its lack of foliage.

Plant bulbocodium in full sun or partial shade in the early fall. It requires only routine garden care.

Left: *Caladium × hortulanum*
Above: *Calochortus venustus*

Caladium

Although this South American tuber does produce small pink flowers, it is grown not for its blooms but for its striking leaves. The heart- or arrow-shaped leaves are veined, edged, or mottled in numerous variations of pink, red, green, silver, and white, and can reach 24 inches in length. The plant itself grows to about 12 inches high.

Caladium × hortulanum, or fancy-leaved caladiums, are popular florist's potted plants. They do best in hot, humid climates and are hardy outdoors only in Zone 10. Elsewhere they must be planted annually and dug up for winter protection, or grown in containers.

Since the tubers will show little growth when temperatures are below 70°F., in warm climates wait to plant until the weather is reliably warm. In the rest of the country, start the tubers indoors about 2 months before you anticipate outdoor temperatures in the 70s. Start the plants in trays of moist peat moss or vermiculite by pressing tubers in 1 to 2 inches deep. Keep the trays between 75°F and 85°F. When leaves appear, transplant into 5- to 7-inch clay pots, or into 4-inch peat pots that can later be set directly in the ground.

Keep evenly moist when in active growth. Cut off leaves as they die. Dig up tubers and store before the first fall frost.

Calochortus (Butterfly Tulip, Cat's Ear, Fairy Lantern, Globe Tulip, Mariposa Lily, Satin Bells)

For a touch of delicate beauty in the bulb garden, add one or more of these American West natives. All bloom in the spring or early summer.

The most popular and colorful of the genus is *Calochortus venustus*, commonly called butterfly tulip or Mariposa lily. Flowers about 4 inches in diameter come in white, yellow, lilac, purple, rose, or red, all with reddish-brown markings. There are tiny hairs at the base of the petals.

C. coeruleus, or cat's ear, is an unusual little lavender cup-shaped flower with fuzzy lining and edges on 3- to 6-inch stems.

Three species bear dainty, globe-shaped flowers that look like tiny lanterns atop delicate stems. *C. albus*, white fairy lantern or satin bell, bears white flowers on 12- to 24-inch stems. The golden fairy lantern, *C. amabilis*, has brown-edged yellow blossoms on 12-inch-tall stems. The purple version, or globe tulip, is *C. amoenus*, with 18- to 24-inch stems displaying mauve-purple flowers.

Except for *C. venustus*, which needs bright sun, plant bulbs in the fall in partial shade. Being western natives, they all need dry summer soil.

Above: *Camassia quamash*
Right: *Canna* hybrid

Bulbs should be dug up after blooming, or else covered with plastic film to prevent excess moisture. All species make attractive houseplants or outdoor potted plants.

Camassia (Camass)

Another hardy bulb native to wet areas of the American West, *Camassia* produces early-spring spikes of small flowers from a clump of narrow leaves. The common camass, *C. quamash*, bears 10 to 40 flowers of blue to white on 30- to 36-inch spikes. *C. cusickii*, known as Cusick camass, bears pale blue flower clusters on 3- to 4-foot spires. *C. leichtlinii*, the Leichtlin camass, produces blue to creamy white flowers on 4-foot spires that twist as the flowers open, and fade from the bottom up.

Camass blooms should be picked when about one-quarter of the flowers in the spike have opened. They will last for up to a week.

You can plant them in the cool fall in any soil, but they prefer heavy soil and ample moisture while growing.

Canna

Cannas, with their broad, tropical-looking, 6- to 12-inch leaves, have spikes of 4- to 5-inch showy flowers in reds, oranges, salmon, apricot, coral, yellows, pinks, and white. Foliage may be bright green or tinged with blue or bronze. Plants may grow from 18 inches to 6 feet tall.

Old-fashioned cannas, *Canna × generalis*, grow to 6 feet or more. For foliage and floral display, however, they cannot rival their modern hybrids, developed in Europe. Among the European improvements are the low-growing and dwarf varieties. These include Pfitzer Dwarfs from Germany, which reach about 2½ to 3 feet in height; the Seven Dwarfs series, which grows to only about half that size; and the Crozy or French cannas, which range from 3 to 4 feet in height and bear huge clusters of flowers. Italian, or orchid-flowered, cannas grow taller and more open in form than the French strains.

Group cannas as accent plants in the garden; be sure their height will not overshadow nearby plantings. Both leaves and flowers are dramatic in arrangements, but the flowers last only for a few days.

Plant in full sunlight and rich soil in the spring in Zones 7 through 10. In colder climates, plant the rhizomes in flats or peat pots indoors about 4 weeks before night temperatures reach 50° to 60°F. While they are actively growing in the garden or containers, apply plenty of moisture and fertilize with a complete fertilizer once or twice a month. North of Zone 7 you will have to dig cannas up every fall, as soon as frost kills the foliage.

Cardiocrinum

In the dense forests of Western and Central China, where the rainfall is the highest in the world, grow the spectacular cardiocrinums. Often found growing side by side with magnolias and rhododendrons, it is understandable why they prefer woodland conditions: moist soil high in organic matter and partial to dense shade. The basal, heart-shaped leaves are a bright, glossy green. Lush trumpet-shaped blossoms up to 6 inches long are among the most fragrant of all bulbs. One species, *Cardiocrinum giganteum*, reaches 12 feet high.

Plant these large bulbs 2 feet apart, as they will yield large plants. They are best in groups of three. Give them a moist, shady spot and rich soil. As they are heavy feeders, it is advisable to work in plenty of fertilizer when planting, which should be done in early fall. Set the bulbs so that the tip is left exposed, above the soil level, but protect it with a deep layer of mulch.

Cardiocrinum is monocarpic, that is the bulb dies after flowering, producing three to five offsets. After the old foliage dies back in the fall, carefully dig the bulb and break off the new offsets; replant them 2 feet apart. As these will take at least 2 years to flower it is best to have new bulbs coming on each year.

Cardiocrinum giganteum grows 10 to 12 feet high, producing up to 20 huge funnel-shaped blossoms that are up to 6 inches long. The trumpets are creamy white, sometimes tinted green; inside, the flowers are striped a purplish color. They bloom in August.

Cardiocrinum giganteum var. *yunnanense* is somewhat smaller. The flowers have no purplish marks inside.

Cardiocrinum cathayanum grows 3 to 4 feet tall. Its white flowers are often shaded with green on the outside, while the throats are spotted with brown. They bloom in early July, with 3 to 5 flowers on each stem.

Cardiocrinum species

Chionodoxa luciliae

Chionodoxa (Glory-of-the-Snow)

These lovely little flowers, known as glory-of-the-snow, originated in the mountains of Asia Minor. Exceptionally hardy, they bloom best in cold climates, blooming right after crocus.

Most popular is *C. luciliae*. The plant sends up 6-inch stems displaying star-shaped blossoms of bright blue with white centers. *C. luciliae* 'Alba' bears all-white flowers and *C. luciliae* 'Rosea' has pink-lilac blossoms. The taller-growing *C. lucilia* 'Gigantea' reaches a height of about 10 inches and produces purple to blue, pink, or white flowers. *C. sardensis* has 6 to 8 deep blue flowers with white throats.

Plant in full sun or partial shade in the early fall. Chionodoxas are so easy to grow that no special attention is necessary. They are ideal for naturalizing and make a wonderful addition to any landscape.

Clintonia (Bluebead Lily)

This charming woodland native is called the bluebead lily for its attractive steel-blue berries that appear in August at the ends of 6- to 8-inch stems. The flowers of *Clintonia borealis* appear in late spring as clusters of small, greenish-yellow bells on erect stems, held above the foliage. The leaves, resembling those of the lily of the valley, are among the few in the bulb world that are attractive all season long.

Clintonia is best grown in cool northern or mountainous climates in moist, acid or slightly acid soil high in organic matter, and in deep to partial shade. Under ideal conditions, *Clintonia* will form large colonies over time. It will not tolerate intense summer sun, and performs as well as any bulb in quite dense shade. It is native from Labrador to Minnesota, south to New Jersey and Indiana.

Fall planting is preferred with this bulb, (actually a rhizome), but it can be moved in spring with considerable success if still dormant. While it can be grown from seed, it is one of the longest-to-flower of all bulbs when raised from seed. Resist the temptation to collect this beauty from the wild, as nursery stock enjoys a much greater rate of transplanting success. When planting, place the rhizome about ½ to 1 inch deep, horizontally, with the new shoot-tip at soil level. Mulch well with a loose cover, such as decaying leaves. Point the tips of the rhizomes in different directions so they can spread outward.

Clintonia umbellata, the speckled bead-lily, is similar to *C. borealis*, but a more southern species, more tolerant of less acidic conditions. Its flowers are greenish-white speckled with green and purple.

Clintonia borealis

Clivia (Kaffir Lily)

South Africa gave the horticultural world the handsome *Clivia miniata*, or kaffir lily. Its foliage looks like other members of the amaryllis family, with clumps of green, strap-shaped leaves growing to 24 inches long. Foot-long stems bear clusters of up to 20 fragrant, yellow-throated, orange flowers outdoors in the spring (in Zones 9 to 10) or—when grown as houseplants—in the winter. Modern hybrids produce flowers in many shades of red, orange, salmon, yellow, and white.

Clivia is often grown in containers even where it is hardy because it produces more flowers when its roots are crowded. Plant bulbs or place pots in shade. Clivia will bloom in deeper shade than most flowers, but like any flower it will bloom better with a bit more light. Keep plants protected by keeping night temperatures above 50°F. all year long.

Clivia miniata

Unlike other bulbs, clivia does not have to be dried off to enforce dormancy. Keep the soil evenly moist all year, reducing the amount to just enough to keep the leaves from wilting when growth slows in the fall. Fertilize with your favorite liquid houseplant food every month during active growth.

Colchicum autumnale

Colchicum (Autumn Crocus, Meadow Saffron)

The unique life cycle of *Colchicum autumnale*, the autumn crocus or meadow saffron, begins shortly after the bulbs are planted in late summer. In autumn, out pop crocuslike flowers in pink, lavender, or white from 2 to 8 inches in diameter. They last a couple of weeks, then disappear. In spring, the plant sends up foliage in the form of bold leaves up to 12 inches long. These last until early summer, then disappear. One species is an exception: *C. luteum* bears yellow flowers in the spring.

Plant colchicums in early fall where they will receive full sun or very light shade and where they can be left alone. One problem is their large foliage, which dominates the area in which they grow. Most people place them in meadow or woodland natural gardens or among shrub plantings where their foliage is less obvious and dominant. The spring-blooming *Colchicum luteum* is hardy only as far north as Zone 7; others are hardy to Zone 3.

Convallaria majalis

Convallaria (Lily-of-the-Valley)

One of the sweetest-smelling of all bulbs is lily-of-the-valley, *C. majalis*. From a pair of 8-inch-long, 2-inch-wide leaves emerges a delicate stem bearing tiny nodding, bell-shaped white blossoms. *C. majalis* 'Rosea' bears pale mauve-pink blooms. Both sometimes produce tiny red-orange berries after blossoming. Cut flowers are beautiful in miniature bouquets and are favorites of brides. Cut them when about a quarter of the spray has opened to make them last longer.

Plant rhizomes in an acid soil and partial shade. Keep them quite moist during the growing season. A fall mulching of compost or well-rotted manure is beneficial.

Unfortunately, *Convallaria* does not grow well in Zones 8 through 10. However, pips (underground shoots sent up by the rhizomes) can be kept in cold storage and forced in containers at any time of the year.

Crinum (Crinum Lily)

Crinum is primarily a tropical and subtropical genus, occasionally planted outdoors in the mildest climates, but more often planted in pots for indoor display. Crinum lilies closely resemble *Amaryllis*.

These are large bulbs that send up long strap-like evergreen leaves and tall, thick stalks with 5 to 10 funnel-shaped flowers up to 3 inches long. *Crinum* × *powellii* is the best hybrid form, and the most readily available. They are excellent to grow in tubs with *Agapanthus*, blooming at the same time, and are hardy to a few degrees of frost, thus can be planted outdoors in mild climates if protected with mulch. *Crinum* × *powellii* produces flowers which open in long succession over a period of several weeks.

Crinum lilies are heavy feeders, so the soil in which they are planted should be well fertilized in advance. Top-dress them each fall with rich compost, and give them an occasional light feeding with liquid fertilizer during the summer.

Set the bulbs so that their necks are just above the soil level. If you are growing them in pots, choose a container 1 inch larger all around than the bulb. Be sure to provide drainage material, such as a 1-inch layer of broken crockery, in the bottom of the pot. For indoor bloom, plant in March and keep at 60°–70°F. to initiate growth. As the bulbs start sending out vegetative growth, provide additional water. When in bloom water frequently. After flowering the plant will go dormant, and will need less water. But remember that crinum lilies are evergreen, and should never be completely dried out.

Crocosmia

While native to South Africa, *Crocosmia* is much hardier than generally supposed, to USDA Zone 5, if protected over winter with mulch. Sometimes listed as *Montbretia*, much hybridizing has been done with this genus, and many cultivars are available. One of the most popular is 'Lucifer', a deep burnt-orange.

From fans of iris-like, sword-shaped leaves arise flower stalks bearing many orange, red, or yellow flowers 1–1½ inches across, in horizontal racemes. Most varieties reach 2 or 3 feet tall. *Crocosmia* will spread into large colonies over time, and in mild climates will reseed readily. It is extremely useful in beds and for splashes of brilliant color, and lasts long as a cut flower.

Crocosmia is best in full sun, although partial shade is tolerated well in hot-summer climates. The soil should be rich and fertile, but very well drained. *Crocosmia* tolerates drought well, and is especially popular in the Mediterranean climate of the west. Easily propagated, the corms multiply rapidly and can be divided for increase. This is best done in early spring while the plants are still dormant. *Crocosmia* blooms in mid- to late summer, depending upon the cultivar.

Crinum species

Crocosmia 'Lucifer'

Crocus hybrid

Crocus

To gardeners and nongardeners alike, the crocus announces the passing of winter. But many people aren't aware that this hardy plant can provide color practically all year round. Although fall-blooming species have no foliage, they offer spots of color between frosts. And gardeners in warm regions enjoy winter-blooming crocuses (actually, premature spring varieties).

These little flowers originated in Asia Minor and southern Europe. All produce 2- to 6-inch stems that bear elongated flowers in white, cream, lavender, lilac, purple, and yellow. The foliage is grassy and often grows to a height of 10 inches. There are so many species and varieties from which to choose that your best bet is to check the current catalog. Select either spring or fall species in any color you desire.

Pick crocuses when the buds have opened enough to show some color. Or, for a longer-lasting display, transplant the corm into a container while it is in flower. You can replant it in the garden when it has finished blooming.

Plant in full sun or partial shade in the early fall. No special attention is necessary. The crocus is a popular winter plant; see page 60.

Cyclamen

Let's look at this genus in two parts: the familiar florist's cyclamen and the smaller, less well-known hardy species. Both are native to the Mediterranean regions of Europe and the Near East. The foliage of cyclamen is almost as pretty as its flowers. Heart-shaped leaves are often marked with pale green, white, or silver. The teardrop-shaped buds open into butterflylike flowers with reflexed petals that turn backward like wings. They hover over the plants on slender brownish-red stems.

The florist's cyclamen, *C. persicum*, is always sold as a potted plant rather than as a tuber. This tender plant produces single, double, fringed, or crested flowers in red, pink, lavender, or white, from late fall through early spring. Plants grow to 10 inches.

Pick fully-opened blossoms by pulling, rather than cutting the flower and its stem from the tuber. Recut the stem ends and immediately sear in a flame.

Below: *Crocus* 'Mr. Pickwick'
Right: *Cyclamen hederifolium*

The hardy cyclamens are much smaller plants, growing to 4 or 5 inches in height, with ¾- to 1-inch flowers. Species bloom in the fall or spring. *C. cilicium*, or Sicily cyclamen, bears pale pink flowers with silver-traced leaves in the fall. *C. coum* is a spring bloomer, with flowers in white, pink, or red. Fall blossoms of the European cyclamen, *C. purpurascens* (formerly called *C. europaeum*), are rose-red and very fragrant, and the foliage is mottled in silver and white. Marbled foliage is also characteristic of late-summer-blooming *C. hederifolium* (formerly known as *C. neapolitanum*), the Neapolitan cyclamen. The rose-pink or white flowers of this fragrant plant bloom before its foliage.

Grow florist's cyclamen in slightly acid soil outdoors in Zones 9 and 10. Transplant into the garden in the fall. In other regions, plant in containers and grow as a houseplant in bright light, but not direct sun. Add ground limestone at a rate of 3 to 5 ounces per bushel to your regular houseplant soil mixture. Feed twice a month with your favorite houseplant fertilizer, and keep the soil quite moist.

Hardy cyclamens grow best in Zones 5 through 9, but can tolerate colder climates if adequately mulched in the winter. In midsummer, plant tubers in partial shade and rich soil.

Dahlia (formal decorative form)

Dahlia (cactus-flowered form)

Dahlia

Modern-day dahlias are far removed from their Mexican ancestors. Hybridizers have found the temptation to create new forms, colors, and sizes irresistible, and the results are mind-boggling. The various cultivars are divided into classifications by size as well as by flower forms. The original dahlias were mild-weather plants; today they can be grown even in Zone 2, provided they get winter protection.

To help you read current catalogs, here is a standard list of dahlia classifications—the first, by flower size; the second, by flower form.

Flower size classification

A: more than 8 inches in diameter
B: 6 to 8 inches
BB: 4 to 6 inches
M: less than 4 inches

Flower form classification

Anemone: Flowers with a row of petals surrounding a dense group of tubular florets.

Ball: Double blooms that are rounded or slightly flattened on top.

Cactus-flowered: Double blooms with many petals, showing no disk; may be incurved toward center, straight, or recurved outward from center.

Colarette: Outer circle of petals surrounding an inner circle of shorter petals, often in different colors.

Dwarf: Small plants and flowers, usually single form.

Decorative: Formal—symmetrically shaped petals; Informal—long, unevenly spaced, often twisted petals.

Mignon: Plants about 18 inches tall with single flowers.

Miniature: Flowers in shape of any other dahlia forms, but on small plants.

Orchid: Star-shaped single flowers with petals that curve backward at end.

Pompon: Miniature versions of the ball form.

Peony: Open centers surrounded by 2 or 3 rows of petals that can be curled or twisted.

Single: Open centers surrounded by a single row of petals that radiate outward.

Plant dahlias in the spring in full sun or partial shade. To flourish, they need plenty of organic matter and supplements of phosphorus and potash. Be sure to dig the soil deeply—to at least a foot below the ground surface.

Top left: *Dahlia* 'Beauty Black'
Top right: *Dahlia* 'Chinese Lantern'
Bottom right: *Dahlia* 'Annette D.'
Above: *Dahlia* 'Fandango'
Above center: *Dahlia* 'Skausen'

Plants are available as tuberous roots or in containers. Plant the latter as you would any other plant; lay the tuberous root on its side in a 7-inch hole, and cover it with 2 inches of soil. Gradually add more soil as the plant grows. When dahlia plants are well established, feed with any complete fertilizer. Provide ample water during the growing season.

You will find it necessary to stake the plants to support the heavy flowers. Many dahlia growers recommend pinching out the center stalks when the plant is small, to produce a sturdier, bushy plant, as well as more flowers. If you wish to grow exhibition-sized blossoms, pinch off all but the terminal buds on side stalks. A second crop of blooms can be grown by pinching back side stalks just one joint from the main stem. All dahlias will flower more profusely if you pick the flowers regularly.

To prevent wilt, plunge cut flower stems into 2 inches of very hot water for about 6 hours. Or, sear the end of the cut stem with the flame of a match or candle. Or, dip cut ends immediately into boiling water for a second or two.

In cold-winter areas dig up dahlias after the tops have been killed by the first hard frost, trim the stem to 6 inches, and allow the tubers to dry for a few hours. Then proceed with winter storage as described on page 78.

Dierama (Fairy Wand)

The rosy, bell-shaped flowers of *Dierama pulcherrimum*, surrounded by papery-white bracts, dangle gracefully from long arching stems, leading to the common name of "angel's fishing rod", or "fairy wand." It is native to eastern South Africa. *Dierama* is easy to grow in mild climate gardens, and in grassy wild meadows, where its slender, grass-like foliage is most at home.

Give *Dierama* well-drained soil. Although it will withstand considerable drought, it will look a lot better with frequent watering during dry spells in summer. Full sun is a must. The mounded, casual foliage and dangling habit of the long "rods" of flowers is particularly effective next to bodies of water. Avoid getting this plant's feet wet, however.

Dierama species

Eranthis (Winter Aconite)

Looking like its buttercup relatives, *Eranthis* (commonly known as winter aconite) covers the ground with sunny yellow flowers that smell like honey. Single blossoms appear very early in the spring, often through the snow, over fine green or bronzed foliage. Two species usually are sold: *E. cilicica* and *E. hyemalis*, both with flowers about 1 inch across. The second is the earlier bloomer and is excellent for naturalizing.

Plant in full sun or partial shade in early fall. Soak the tubers in water for 24 hours before planting in any soil that doesn't get too dry during summer months.

Eranthis hyemalis

Eremurus (Desert-Candle, Foxtail Lily)

One of the most dramatic summer flowers is the foxtail lily or desert-candle. Spikes of bell-like flowers tower to 8 feet, growing from a rosette of sword-like leaves. The long-lasting flower spike opens from the bottom upward.

Eremurus stenophyllus (formerly *E. bungei*) bears yellow flowers on a 3- to 4-foot spike. *E. elwesii* bears pink flowers on a 6- to 9-foot spike, and *E. himalaicus* produces white blooms on a 3- to 6-foot spike. The giant foxtail lily, *E. robustus*, is the tallest (8 to 10 feet) and bears pink blossoms. The Shelford Hybrids are shorter (3 to 4 feet), with flowers in rose, peach, orange, yellow, cream, or white.

Plant tuberous roots during fall in full sun, giving each plenty of room. Handle them gently to prevent breakage. Mulch in fall to protect the roots. When you want additional plants in the garden, purchase new rootstocks; foxtail lilies do not thrive when disturbed.

Eremurus robustus

Erythronium (Adder's Tongue, Dog-Tooth Violet, Easter Bells, Trout Lily, Fawn Lily)

The best-known species is a European native, *Erythronium dens-canis*. Its common name, dog-tooth violet, has nothing to do with the appearance of the flower, but with that of the corm. The delicate flower is purple or rose colored, rising from mottled leaves on a 6-inch stem.

The other species, many of them with mottled foliage, are natives of the North American woodlands. They're known by several descriptive names, most commonly fawn lily (because of the foliage) or trout lily, adder's-tongue, or Easter bells. *E. grandiflorum* has plain green foliage and 24-inch stems with yellow blossoms. *E. citrinum* also bears yellow flowers, but the stems are only 8 inches tall.

The others grow to a height of about 12 inches, with the following flowers: *E. albidum*, white to light blue; *E. americanum*, yellow tinged with pink; *E. californicum*, creamy white or yellow; *E. hendersonii*, purple; *E. oregonum*, creamy white; *E. revolutum*, creamy to purple; and *E. tuolumnense*, yellow with greenish base. All bloom in the spring, and many have a delicate fragrance.

Plant in shade or partial shade in warm areas, or in sun where summers

Erythronium americanum

Eucharis grandiflora

are cooler. Plant during fall in moist, well-drained soil. *Erythronium* will need moisture all summer long even though dormant, and it does not like extreme heat. Fall mulching offers sufficient protection in cold regions.

Eucharis (Amazon Lily, Lily-of-the-Amazon, Madonna Lily)

Eucharis grandiflora (sometimes called *E. amazonica*), or the Amazon lily, is an evergreen that may bloom at any time of the year. Fragrant flowers are pure white, about 2 inches wide, and look much like a daffodil, except that several are borne on a stalk.

Due to its tropical origins, *Eucharis* is very tender. It is normally grown in containers, even in warm climates, because it blooms better when its roots are crowded.

Plant 3 to 4 bulbs per 8-inch clay pot in any good houseplant mixture, adding ground limestone at the rate of 3 to 5 ounces per bushel. Place in bright light, but not direct sun, in a warm place where night temperatures stay above 65°F. Keep moist and apply houseplant fertilizer every 2 weeks while the bulbs are in active growth. After they have bloomed, fertilize and water only enough to keep leaves from wilting. When evidence of renewed growth is seen, resume normal watering and feeding.

Freesia

The sweet smell of freesia blossoms in winter or early spring is one of the headiest pleasures of gardening. The plant is grassy, with long, slender leaves. Each wiry, 12- to 18-inch-long stem bears 5 to 10 trumpet-shaped flowers. *Freesia armstrongii* produces pink flowers; *F. refracta*, either white or yellow. Modern hybrids, the result of crossing the two, run the gamut: purple, lavender, lilac, mauve, blue, pink, red, orange, rust, and yellow. However, some of the hybrids are less fragrant than either of their parents.

Cut freesias when the first couple of flowers in the spray are open. The buds will open, one by one, right up to the tip. During fall in Zones 9 and 10, plant freesia corms directly in the garden in bright sun. Keep moist and feed monthly until color buds appear.

In Zones 1 through 8, specially treated freesia corms from the Netherlands can be planted in the spring to bloom in midsummer. Dig the corms after the foliage ripens. Store them until fall, and plant as houseplants. Start with more treated corms again each year for the outdoor garden.

Freesias grown as houseplants should be planted during fall in a mixture of 2 parts loam and 1 part perlite or coarse sand. For a succession of blooms, plant every two weeks through December. Plants benefit from addition of ground limestone to the soil. Place pots outside until just before the first frost; then move them inside to a cool spot where they will get plenty of sun. A temperature of about 55°F. is ideal. Water and fertilize as for outdoor freesias. After the foliage withers, remove corms from pots and store in a dry place until fall.

Fritillaria (Checkered Lily, Crown Imperial, Guinea-Hen Tulip, Snake's Head)

Exotic is the word for this genus's flowers. Only two species are commonly grown in most American bulb gardens. The crown imperial, *Fritillaria imperialis*, sends up a 2½-to 4-foot stem in spring, with broad leaves growing all the way up the stalk, as with lilies. At the top is a tuft of leaves, under which hangs a cluster of 2-inch, musky-smelling flowers in yellow, red, or orange. Plant the crown imperial in an unobtrusive garden spot where the odor won't be objectionable.

F. meleagris, known by such descriptive names as snake's-head, guinea-hen tulip, or checkered lily, grows to about 12 inches in spring. Its bell-shaped flowers look like checkered purple-and-white fabric-covered lampshades, and are about 1½ to 2 inches long. Because this flower does not

Top left: *Freesia* hybrids
Bottom left: *Fritillaria imperialis*
Bottom right: *Fritillaria meleagris* (variety 'Alba' on the left)

have the musky odor of the crown imperial, it is a better choice for a cut flower. Variety 'Alba' is pure white.

Additionally, a number of fritillarias are native to the American Northwest and seem to grow well only there. Gardeners in that area may choose late-winter- to late-spring-flowering *F. lanceolata*, the checker lily. Its bowl-shaped bells are brown to purple and mottled with greenish yellow and purple. Another spring bloomer is *F. pudica*, with yellow to orange bell-shaped flowers that become deep red as they mature. *F. recurva* bears bright red bells with yellow flecks on the inside and purple tinges on the outside. Plant during early fall—in full sun for the crown imperial, in filtered shade for the others. The large bulbs of the crown imperial are best planted laid on their side to prevent water collecting in the hollow at the top of the bulb. Fertilize with a complete fertilizer when growth begins in the spring. *E. imperialis* does well in Zones 5 through 8; *F. meleagris*, in Zones 3 through 8.

Top: *Galanthus nivalis*
Below: *Galtonia candicans*

Galanthus (Snowdrops)

Little white-flowered snowdrops are one of the very first bulbs to appear in early spring or late winter. Two species are offered by bulb distributors. *Galanthus elwesii*, or giant snowdrop, bears flowers on 12-inch stems above 8-inch-long leaves. Blue-green foliage characterizes *G. nivalis*, the common snowdrop, with flowers borne on 6- to 9-inch stems. Bell-shaped flowers of both species are waxy, with green tips on the inner segments.

Plant during early fall or late summer in partial shade or full sun. No special care is necessary, and you should not have to bother about *Galanthus* for years.

Gladiolus tristis

Galtonia (Summer Hyacinth)

Known as the spire lily, *Galtonia candicans* produces tall, 4-to 5-foot leafless flower stalks above a rosette of long, straplike basal leaves. The flowers appear at the tops of the stalks as drooping bells in open clusters. Blooming in late summer, it is an excellent addition to the rear of the border in combination with Michaelmas daisies. The flowers usually keep appearing until early fall. While this plant is from South Africa, it is quite hardy (USDA Zone 5).

As *Galtonia* is a heavy feeder, give it rich, well-fertilized soil when first planting, and feed occasionally with weak liquid fertilizer during the growing season. The bulbs are best planted in the spring in groups of 6, 1 foot apart and 6 inches deep. Spread a layer of sand at the bottom of each hole to ensure good drainage. Especially in cold areas, these bulbs should be protected with a deep layer of mulch over winter.

Galtonia make an excellent cut flower, lasting long in the vase, and they are extremely fragrant.

Gladiolus

The gladiolus has long been a favorite in the florist trade for the aristocratic beauty it brings to arrangements. But it also lends an air of dramatic beauty to the garden.

Gladiolus leaves are sword-shaped and surround spikes that bear funnel-shaped flowers. Most of the gladiolus bulbs now available are modern hybrids bred for big flowers in a vast color range. Some growers offer a few species of gladioli as well.

Small-flowering glads are becoming more available and increasingly more popular. These include the baby, miniature, and butterfly hybrids, as well as *Gladiolus* species. Among the species available are: *G. carneus* (formerly *G. blandus*), with red flowers on spikes 12 to 18 inches in height; *G. byzantinus*, another red-flowering glad that grows to 24 inches; *G. tristis*, whose creamy to yellow flowers on spikes about 18 inches tall offer nighttime fragrance; and red-and-yellow *G.* × *colvillei*, which is reputed to be the first hybrid introduced, and which grows to 18 inches.

Large-flowering hybrids, *G.* × *hortulanus*, come in almost any color you can name. They're classified by size, and the catalogs identify them by means of series numbers.

Flower size classification

Miniature (100 Series): Flowers less than 2 inches across.
Small (200 Series): Flowers between 2 and 3 inches across.
Medium (300 Series): Flowers between 3 and 4 inches across.
Large (400 Series): Flowers between 4 and 5 inches across.
Giant (500 Series): Flowers greater than 5 inches across. Some get as large as 8 inches and are borne on spikes up to 6 feet tall.

Cut glads when the first bottom flower is fully opened. Most of the remaining buds will open a few at a time, almost to the tip. Pick the faded flowers and cut the stem each day to avoid a leggy look in the arrangement.

Left: *Gladiolus* hybrids
Right: *Gloriosa rothschildiana*

If you place a gladiolus stalk at an angle in a vase, it will curve upward in a few hours and add grace and interest to your arrangement.

Plant gladioli in full sun as soon as possible after the last frost. To have a succession of blooms, plant corms every 2 weeks, up until 2 months before the first frost is anticipated. Fertilize when the flower spikes first appear and after the flowers are picked. Water heavily.

To keep stalks erect, either stake and tie them, or mound earth around the stem to a height of 6 inches.

Gladiolus hybrids are hardy in Zones 8 through 10; and some species glads, as far north as Zone 5. Whatever your growing zone, however, they will all be far more productive if dug up each year after the foliage dies.

Dig corms while the stems are still attached; then cut back stems to within 1 inch of the corm. (Twisting off the stem can injure the corm.) Dry corms in the sun for an afternoon and then cure them for about 2 weeks where air can circulate freely around them. They needn't be kept cool during the curing period. Remove the stems, old corms, and husks and store in sawdust- or vermiculite-filled flats or in paper bags in a cool (40° to 50°F.) place.

Gloriosa (Climbing Lily, Glory Lily)

A native of tropical Africa, glory lily, *Gloriosa rothschildiana*, is also known as climbing lily because it supports itself by attaching its leaf-tip tendrils to trellises or other structures. Summer flowers are bright red with golden banding along the wavy edges of the petals. Its form is the traditional lily shape.

Cut the flowers when they have opened almost all the way. They will last about 5 days.

Gloriosa can be grown as a houseplant indoors, as a greenhouse specimen, or outdoors in the garden. For early outdoor bloom in cool climates, start the tubers in containers indoors in the soil mixture recommended on page 68. When the weather is warm, transplant or move outdoors in pots. No matter where you grow *Gloriosa*, position it in full sunlight and provide string, wire, or a trellis on which it can climb. Feed with liquid fertilizer every 3 weeks. Keep evenly moist until dormancy begins in fall. Store the plant in its container, or dig up the tubers and store.

Hippeastrum (Amaryllis)

Hippeastrum is commonly known as amaryllis. This frequently causes confusion, since *Amaryllis* is the botanical name of another genus. (See page 87). In warm climates it can be planted in the ground outdoors, but it mainly is grown as a houseplant, particularly around the winter holidays.

Clusters of 3 to 6 huge, lilylike flowers to 10 inches in diameter are borne on a thick 12- to 24-inch stalk. The stalks grow so fast you can almost see them lengthen. Long 1½- to 2-foot strap-shaped leaves can precede or follow the flower stalk, or both may appear simultaneously. Often a second flower stalk appears. Almost all cultivated plants are hybrids. Flower colors include white, pink, coral, salmon, rose, red, and stripes of these colors. The species *H. calyptrata* has green flowers.

Pot bulbs in late fall to early spring in a good houseplant mix. The pot should have at least 2 inches of space on all sides of the bulb. Plant so that half the bulb is exposed above the soil. You can create an impressive effect by planting several in a large container. Water well after potting, then wait until the flower stalk appears before watering again.

Position the plant where it will get several hours of direct or bright indirect sun each day. Keep it evenly moist, and feed monthly with your favorite liquid fertilizer for houseplants. The leaves will yellow and wither in late summer. At that point withhold water and let the bulb rest in an out-of-the way place for a few weeks. About 6 weeks before you want more blooms, wash out some of the old soil and add a fresh mixture. Water well and place in the light again. Repot every few years.

Hippeastrum hybrid

Hyacinthus (Hyacinth)

The distinct perfume of the spring-blooming hyacinth is a familiar pleasure to most flower lovers. One stalk in a pot or arrangement can easily scent an entire room.

The most widely grown hyacinths are the Dutch cultivars of the single species *Hyacinthus orientalis*, the common hyacinth. These cultivars, which have been grown in gardens for hundreds of years, are larger and more densely flowered than the original species. The original colors of the com-

Hyacinthus orientalis

Above: *Hymenocallis narcissiflora*
Right: *Hyacinthus orientalis*

mon hyacinth flowers are white, pale blue, or purplish, to which have been added pink, red, royal purple, dark blue, and yellow. Bulbs are rated in the Netherlands by size: miniatures are 14 to 15 centimeters (5½ inches) in circumference; exhibition size is more than 19 centimeters (7½ inches) in circumference.

A natural variety of the species that grows in southern France, the Roman hyacinth, *H. orientalis* var. *albulus*, produces white flowers much more loosely around a more slender stalk. Several stalks rise from each bulb.

Cut hyacinths when most of the buds have opened. They will stay fresh for about 5 days.

Plant the bulbs in rich soil in full sun during early fall in colder regions and during late fall to early winter in warm climates.

H. orientalis var. *albulus* is not hardy north of Zone 6; others are hardy through Zone 4. In the colder regions of these zones, apply winter mulch.

Hyacinths are popular for forcing (see page 62).

Hymenocallis (Basket Flower, Peruvian Daffodil, Spider Lily)

Plants of *Hymenocallis narcissiflora* (sometimes listed as *H. calathina* or *Ismene calathina*) have strap-shaped leaves much like those of the amaryllis. In summer, 2-foot stems shoot up from the basal clump, topped by clusters of 2 to 4 complex, fragrant white flowers with green stripes. The flower form gives the bulb its common names of Peruvian daffodil, spider lily, or basket flower. The cultivar 'Sulphurea' has yellow flowers.

Hymenocallis is hardy in Zones 8 through 10 and can be planted in fall or spring in full sun. Elsewhere, plant after the last spring frost and dig up before the first fall frost. Spider lilies may also be grown in pots and treated as houseplants or greenhouse plants; when night temperatures are above 60°F., you can move the pots to the patio or the garden if you wish. Houseplant spider lilies will stay evergreen year round, and during the winter should be watered only enough to keep the foliage from withering.

Hypoxis (Star Grass)

While most of the members of this genus are tropical, *Hypoxis hirsuta* is a hardy native of the midwestern United States. *Hypoxis* is a small plant, growing 4 to 8 inches tall, and producing narrow, strap-like leaves that are often hairy. The flowers are yellow on the inside, light green on the exterior

Hypoxis hirsuta

of the petals, about ¾ of an inch in diameter, and are borne on loosely branched heads. They bloom in late spring or early summer.

Star grass must have a gritty, well-drained soil that is kept evenly moist. Species other than *H. hirsuta* should be grown in a cool greenhouse in pans or shallow pots; an alpine house is ideal. *H. hirsuta* may be grown outdoors as far north as Boston. Due to their small size and partiality for gritty soil, they are especially well-suited to the rock garden.

Above: Bearded iris

Below far left: Siberian irises, from left, 'Vi Luihn', 'Fourfold White', 'Sparkling Rose', and 'Big Blue' (bottom).

Clockwise from middle top: Spuria Irises 'Sierra Nevada', 'Conquista', 'Protégé', 'Sierra Nevada'.

Iris

Irises are one of the most complex groups of plants in the bulb garden. Hobbyists devote long hours to their study and identification, and so many new cultivars are introduced each year that only the experts can keep up with the changes. For the sake of simplicity, irises can be divided into two major groups: **beardless** (apogon) and **bearded** (pogon). Many taxonomists today recommend classifying these groups as two separate genera.

The swordlike leaves of all irises are similar. Flowers are in 6 segments; the 3 inner segments (standards) are usually smaller than the outer petals and stand erect; the 3 outer segments (falls) are reflexed, extending outward or downward.

Cut beardless irises when one flower has opened; cut bearded iris as the first bud is opening and let it open fully inside the house.

Beardless irises. Beardless irises have smooth falls, without beards. Some of these are rhizomatous, others are bulbous.

Beardless irises with rhizomes. Japanese irises bloom in mid- to late summer in shades of white, blue, purple, and pink, with both single and double flower forms. **Louisiana irises** are native to that area. Yellow spears on each sepal contrast with the flower color of white, pink, reddish, purple, blue, or yellow. The **butterfly iris,** or **Spuria** group, produces delicate-looking late spring blooms in white, yellow, bronze, brown, blue, lavender, and many combinations of these. Many are splotched or veined with markings reminiscent of butterfly wings. **Siberian irises** also bear butterfly-type flowers in shades of purple, blue, red, or white.

Left: A 3-year-old clump of Siberian iris.

Iris sibirica 'Sparkle'

Dutch iris

Iris reticulata

Plant rhizomes of all these in late summer. With the exception of spuria and Siberian irises, which must have excellent drainage, beardless irises require plenty of moisture; the rhizomes must never completely dry out, even when being transplanted. Japanese irises are frequently planted in containers and submerged in water gardens while in active growth and bloom. They prefer partial shade, as do the Louisiana irises; however, both these groups need full sun when grown in regions cooler than their native habitats. Siberian and spuria irises should be planted in full sun. Japanese, Louisiana, and Siberian irises prefer acid soil, but adapt to any soil if acid fertilizer is applied in the spring and at planting time. Spuria irises will not bloom well in cool or wet climates. Most of these irises adapt to cooler climates if given adequate root protection in winter.

Beardless irises with bulbs. Irises that grow from true bulbs include the reticulata group and the Dutch irises.

The **Reticulatas** are low-growing, early spring-blooming bulbs that reach heights of only 4 to 8 inches. Foliage is delicate and grassy. Blooms appear in purple, violet, blue, yellow, or white, and most have yellow markings on their falls. Species include *I. bakerana* in deep purple, *I. danfordiae*, in yellow, *I. histrioides* 'Major' in blue, and *I. reticulata* in deep violet, with hybrids in several hues.

Today's **Dutch irises** are hybrids of the Spanish iris, *I. xiphium*, and several other species. Their flowers are reminiscent of orchids, in hues of white, purple, blue, violet, and yellow. They flower in the spring.

Plant the true bulb irises during fall in full sun and well-drained soil. Water generously during active growth. Provide winter mulching in cool zones. Both Dutch and reticulatas make excellent container-grown plants if they are protected against freezing.

Bearded irises. Extensive hybridization over many years has resulted in a huge number of cultivars of the bearded iris. Their growth habit is rhizomatous. This large and most important group of garden irises are distinguished by a fuzzy "beard," or hairy filaments, growing in the center of the fall. The vast range of colors and color combinations have resulted in a

Above: *Iris* 'Cranberry Ice' (tall bearded self)
Above right: *Iris* (tall bearded)

specialized terminology for the plant. Generally, the flowers are divided into five categories:

1. A *self* is a flower with solid, uniform color.
2. A *plicata* is generally white or yellow, with contrasting "freckles," or mottling.
3. A *bicolor* has standards of one color and falls of another, usually darker color. Bicolors have several subclasses, including: *amoenas*, which have white standards and colored falls; *reverse amoenas*, with white falls and colored standards; and *variegatas*, which have yellow standards and falls of purple, red, or brown.
4. *Bitones* have standards of one color, and falls of a different value of the same color.
5. *Blends*, the last category, are varieties with two or more colors variously intergraded in the same flower parts.

These five categories of flower coloration are applicable to all classes of bearded iris. These "classes" have been divided into four major groups; the first three that follow are organized around size.

Iris 'Snow Mound' (tall bearded amoena)

Tall bearded iris. Tall bearded irises have far surpassed their ancestors. Branched stems reach heights to 4 feet and bear dramatic flowers. Many are ruffled. They are available in almost any color, and their petals may be veined or marked with other hues.

Median iris. These offspring of the Tall Bearded group include the **border iris** with bloomstalks that grow to 25 inches, and slightly smaller flowers than the tall bearded group. **Intermediate bearded irises** have flowers similar to the tall group, but range in height from 15 to 28 inches. **Miniature tall bearded irises** grow to 25 inches and have 2½- to 3½-inch flowers, while **standard dwarf bearded irises** grow to heights of 10 to 15 inches.

Clockwise from top left: *Iris* 'Camelot Rose' (tall bearded bicolor); 'Cozy Calico' (tall bearded plicata); a tall bearded iris with ruffled edges; an intermediate bearded plicata; 'Victoria Falls' (tall bearded self); 'Brown Doll', 'Dresden Candleglow', 'Tamino' (intermediate bearded).

Top: Dwarf bearded irises 'VIM + 60' (left) and 'Fortune Cookie' (right).

Above left: *Iris cristata* 'Witt'

Above right: *Iris* 'Little Buccaneer' (dwarf bearded)

Below: *Iris* 'Bee Wings' (dwarf bearded)

Miniature dwarf bearded iris. These dwarfs range from 3 to 10 inches in height, with flowers that mimic their larger counterparts.

Aril and arilbred iris. Aril irises consist of two groups, **Oncocyclus** and **Regelia irises**. As these come from the deserts of the Middle East, they are difficult to grow in most North American gardens. Arilbreds are hybrids of the arils and other bearded irises. These are easier to grow than their desert ancestors, but they retain many of the interesting colors and exotic patterns of the arils.

Because of their desert heritage, arils and arilbreds are susceptible to rot and bacterial diseases. Therefore, the rhizomes should be dug and divided every year. They need lots of moisture during active growth, but must be dried completely in midsummer—the combination of heat and excess moisture encourages rhizome diseases.

Plant or transplant all bearded irises during late summer in full sun, and provide excellent drainage. Heavier soils are preferred to sandy ones. Fertilize when planting, and before and after flowering, with plant food high in phosphorus. Continue to water for about 6 weeks after flowering; then let the soil dry out between waterings into the fall. Remove dead leaves, but do not cut back green foliage. Divide clumps every 3 to 5 years.

Crested iris. Crested irises fall somewhere between bearded and beardless in appearance. All are rhizomatous in growth habit and have linear crests at the base of their falls. Check garden catalogs for *I. cristata, I. gracilipes, I. tectorum,* and *I. japonica*. Crested irises differ from most other irises in that they can be grown in the shade. Except for *I. cristata* and *I. gracilipes*, most are not hardy in cool climates, but they make interesting additions to the warm greenhouse when grown in containers.

Ixia (African Corn Lily)

African corn lilies flower freely in late spring or early summer with brilliantly colored, cup-shaped blooms in red, pink, orange, yellow, and creamy white. These are clustered atop strong, thin stems that can reach 1½ to 2 feet in height. On sunny days the 2-inch flowers open flat, displaying their contrasting centers. Foliage is grassy and swordlike.

Plant *Ixia* in full sun during the fall. It is hardy in Zones 8 through 10, but can be grown in Zones 6 and 7 if winter protection is adequate; however, container culture is best in cooler climates. Like *Gladiolus*, *Ixia* corms will flower better if dug and stored during summer and replanted each fall.

Cut *Ixia* flowers when the second flower on a spike has opened all the way. The spike will keep providing new flowers for 10 days.

Ixia hybrid

Ixiolirion (Lily-of-the-Altai, Siberian Lily, Sky-Blue Lily)

The dainty violet-blue flowers of *Ixiolirion tataricum* (formerly *I. montanum* or *I. pallasii*) look like open hyacinths and are borne on 12- to 16-inch weak stems over sparse foliage. They bloom profusely in late spring and make long-lasting cut flowers.

Plant in full sun during fall in warm zones. Wait until after spring frosts to plant from Zone 6 north. No special attention is necessary.

Ixiolirion tataricum

Leucojum (Snowflakes)

Snowflakes are among the easier bulbs to grow. The three species commonly cultivated bloom at different times. Earliest to bloom is *Leucojum vernum*, or spring snowflake, with single, bell flowers tipped in green on 6- to 9-inch stems. Slightly larger and bearing 4 to 8 similar blossoms per stem is the summer snowflake, *L. aestivum*. In early fall the autumn snowflake, *L. autumnale*, appears. Its blossoms are pinkish, and there are usually 2 or 3 on each of the 4- to 6-inch stems. All snowflake bulbs send out several grassy leaves.

Plant in full sun or partial shade in the fall. No special care is necessary, and the bulbs flower best if left undisturbed for several years at a time. The fall snowflake does not do well in warm climates.

Leucojum aestivum

Lilium (Easter Lily, Lily, Madonna Lily)

Nothing growing in the landscape surpasses a clump or mass of lilies for beauty. Up close, no single flower could be more magnificent or regal. Lilies look as though they should be much more difficult to grow than they actually are. Today's lilies are a vast improvement over the original species because of disease resistance, vigorous growth, profuse flowering, ease of culture, and self-propagation. You can choose lilies to provide a succession of blooms from spring well into fall.

Lilium is a complex genus. Thanks to the North American Lily Society and the Royal Horticultural Society of England, lilies have been classified according to types. Perhaps the descriptions that follow will make your lily bulb-shopping easier.

Asiatic hybrids. Early flowering, these grow 2 to 5 feet in height, with 4- to 6-inch compact flowers in reds, pinks, oranges, yellows, lavender, and white.

Upright-flowering. Mid-Century Hybrids, 'Enchantment', 'Golden Chalice', and 'Harmony'.

Outward-facing. 'Corsage', 'Paprika', and 'Prosperity'.

Pendant-flowering. 'Citronella', Harlequin Hybrids, and 'Sonata'.

Martagon hybrids. Late-spring-flowering; 3 to 6 feet in height, with 3- to 4-inch flowers in white, yellow, lavender, orange, brown, lilac, tangerine, and mahogany. Includes Paisley Hybrids.

Above: *Lilium* 'Redbird' (Oriental hybrid)
Right: *Lilium* 'Love Song'
Far right top: *Lilium* 'Crimson Beauty'
Far right bottom: Hybrid *Lilium speciosum* 'Candlestick Lily × *L. philadelphicum* var. *andinum*

Candidum hybrids. Late-spring- and early-summer-flowering; 3 to 4 feet in height with 4- to 5-inch flowers. Hybrids resulting from crosses between *L. candidum* and *L. chalcedonicum*. Plant in fall, only 1 or 2 inches deep.

American hybrids. Late-spring- and early-summer-flowering; 4 to 8 feet in height with 4- to 6-inch flowers. Hybrids of North American native lilies, including the Bellingham Hybrids and San Gabriel Strain.

Aurelian hybrids. Summer-flowering; 4 to 6 feet tall with 6- to 10-inch flowers. Includes the Trumpet Hybrids such as 'Pink Perfection', 'Black Dragon', and 'Golden Splendor'; Bowl-shaped Hybrids such as 'Heart's Desire'; Pendant Hybrids such as 'Golden Showers'; and Sunburst Hybrids, including 'Golden Sunburst' and 'Lightning'.

Longiflorum hybrids. The familiar white Easter lily or white trumpet lily, *L. longiflorum*, and hybrids. Forced for sale at Easter; normally bloom midsummer.

Oriental hybrids. Late-summer-flowering; 2 to 8 inches in height with flowers to 12 inches. Bowl-shaped flowers include 'Empress of India', 'Little Rascal', and 'Red Baron'. Flat-faced flowers with recurving petals include hybrids of *L. speciosum* and *L. auratum*, such as the Imperial Strains 'Imperial Gold', 'Jamboree', and 'Imperial Silver'.

Species lilies. Includes long-grown species native to North America, Europe, and Asia. Heights from 2 to 6 feet and blooming time from spring into fall. Outstanding species for American gardens include *L. auratum* (from Japan), with huge white flowers banded in yellow and spotted in reddish-brown; *L. candidum* (from the Near East), the white Madonna lily; *L. regale* (from western China), the regal lily with large white trumpet-shaped blooms; *L. speciosum* (from Japan), large fragrant lilies in white or red; and *L. martagon* (from Asia), the Turk's-cap lily with pink blooms.

Unclassified hybrids. A special category for yet-to-be-developed hybrids that may not fall into any of the previous groups.

Left: Lilium 'Jamboree' (Oriental hybrid)
Top right: *Lilium* (Houghton hybrid)
Above: *Lilium* 'Shooting Star'

Most lilies will last for a week as cut flowers. If falling pollen detracts from the beauty of the petals, either remove the anthers with a pair of scissors or brush the ripe pollen from the anthers daily.

Plant lilies during spring or fall in full sun, although some will do well in very light shade. They need lots of moisture during active growth, but they cannot tolerate wet soil, and thus they require excellent drainage. Fertilize when the plants appear in spring, and regularly thereafter until the foliage begins to yellow. If wind is a problem, stake the plants. Lilies can be left in the ground year-round as far north as Zone 3. In warm climates, plant precooled bulbs, or dig the bulbs after the foliage has died and refrigerate them for 2 months before replanting.

Any lily can be grown in a container outdoors, but for indoor cultivation choose the more compact Mid-Century Hybrids or the Easter lily. Place the precooled bulb near the bottom of a standard pot (not a bulb pan). Put the pot in a cool spot, keep the soil evenly moist during growth, and feed the plant monthly with any liquid houseplant fertilizer until the buds begin to show color. Withhold water when the leaves wither. Plant the bulbs in the garden after they have bloomed.

Lycoris squamigera

Lycoris (Amaryllis, Hurricane Lily, Magic Lily of Japan, Naked Lady, Resurrection Lily, Spider Lily, Yellow Spider)

The strap-shaped leaves of this plant appear in the spring, then die away by late summer. They're followed shortly by stems up to 2 feet tall with late-summer to early-fall clusters of flowers in pink, white, red, or yellow. Recurved segments and long, curled stamens give them their common name of spider lily.

The yellow spider is *Lycoris africana* (often sold as *L. aurea*); *L. radiata* (sometimes listed as *Amaryllis radiata*) blooms in pink to scarlet. *L. radiata* 'Alba' is white. Pink or rosy-lilac flowers are produced by *L. squamigera* (formerly *Amaryllis hallii*), commonly known as hurricane lily, naked lady, hardy amaryllis, resurrection lily, or the magic lily of Japan.

Cut *Lycoris* flowers when the cluster is half open. They will keep for about 10 days.

Plant *Lycoris* during late summer or fall in full sun or partial shade. *L. squamigera* is hardy as far north as Zone 5, but the others are warm-climate species. All *Lycoris* grow well anywhere in containers, since they flower more abundantly when their roots are crowded. Treat *Lycoris* slightly differently from other container-grown bulbs. Water well when you plant, but wait until stalks appear before watering again. Water while they are in bloom, then withhold moisture until foliage appears. Resume watering and feed with liquid houseplant fertilizer. When the foliage begins to ripen, however, water *very* sparingly (the soil should be nearly dry) until flower stalks appear once again.

Moraea (Butterfly Iris, Fortnightly Lily, Peacock Iris)

Warm-climate gardeners derive much pleasure from these year-round evergreen plants that, in the absence of frost, bloom constantly. An unusual characteristic is the later appearance of additional blooms on stems that have previously blossomed.

Two species, *Moraea tricuspidata* and *M. neopavonia* (often called *Iris pavonia*), are commonly called peacock iris because the larger outer petals of their yellow flowers are marked like the end of peacock feathers. A variety, *M. neopavonia villosa*, flowers in purple, red, yellow, or white. The plants of

Dietes vegata

these species look like iris, and the 2- to 4-inch flowers stand on stems that are 1½ to 3 feet in height.

A closely related genus *Dietes* is often included with *Moraea*. *D. bicolor* (known also as *M. bicolor* or *Iris bicolor*) is called yellow moraea. Its 2-inch flowers are marked with a brownish spot at the base of each of the 3 outer petals.

Butterfly iris and fortnightly lily are common names for *D. vegata* (also often listed as *M. iridoides*). It sports white flowers spotted with brownish yellow and purplish blue.

In warm, practically frost-free climates, plant moraea outdoors in full sun. *D. bicolor* needs moist soil; the others prefer it dry. Set out the plants any time during the year.

In most climates you'll choose to grow moraea as an indoor plant. Indoors it needs 4 hours of direct sun each day, and night temperatures that stay above 60°F. Pot it in the mixture recommended on page 68. Keep the soil evenly moist, and fertilize monthly.

Muscari armeniacum

Muscari (Grape Hyacinth)

The clear blue of grape hyacinths can enhance the spring garden or, when forced, brighten up a winter day indoors. Foliage is grassy and often untidy in the garden. The bell flowers are borne in clusters all around the stem. Their fragrance is delightfully sweet.

Blossoms of *Muscari armeniacum*, or Armenian grape hyacinth, are bright blue on 4- to 8-inch stems. The cultivar 'Early Giant' is very popular.

M. botryoides, the Italian grape hyacinth, flowers in deep blue on 6- to 12-inch stems. Look for the white cultivar 'Album'.

M. tubergenianum is sometimes called Oxford and Cambridge grape hyacinth because it produces bells that are dark blue at the top of its 8-inch stem and lighter blue at the bottom.

Not all grape hyacinths are blue, however. Musk grape hyacinth, *M. racemosum* (often called *M. moschatum*), is purple.

The most unusual species is *M. comosum*, which bears green-fringed purplish flowers on 8- to 12-inch stems. The cultivar 'Monstrosum', called the feather hyacinth, has fuzzy mauve-blue blossoms.

Flowers will keep for about 5 days. Cut them when the spike is half opened.

Grape hyacinths are among the easiest bulbs to grow. Plant them in the early fall in full sun or partial shade. Routine garden care is all they require. Plant in pots for outdoor gardening or indoor blooms (see pages 68–70).

Narcissus (Angel's Tears, Daffodil, Jonquil)

Without doubt, daffodils, jonquils, narcissus, or whatever you choose to call them are the world's favorite bulb. These natives of the Mediterranean area, central Europe, Japan, and China have become so interbred that confusion exists over names, parentage, and classification. But by any name, these cheerful, often fragrant flowers play important roles in the landscape, container gardens indoors and out, and bouquets.

The divisions designated by The Royal Horticultural Society of England come in handy when looking at the vast genus *Narcissus*.

Trumpet daffodils. These have one flower per stem in yellow, white, and bicolors, with the trumpet as long as or longer than the petals. An old favorite is 'King Alfred'.

Large-cupped daffodils. Again, there is one flower per stem, with trumpets more than a third the size of (but less than equal to the length of) the petals.

Color groups. Yellow petals with yellow or orange cup; white petals with any color cup; white petals with white cup; and other colors such as pink or orange.

Above: Narcissus 'King Alfred' (trumpet daffodil)

Top right: *Narcissus* 'Cheerfulness' (double narcissus)

Bottom right: *Narcissus* 'Pink Punch' (large-cupped daffodil)

Below: *Narcissus* 'California Giant' (cyclamineus hybrid)

Small-cupped daffodils. These have one flower per stem, with the cup not more than a third the length of the petals. Color groups are the same as for the large-cupped group.

Double narcissus. Stems have any number of flowers; all types have more than one layer of petals. Grows in white, yellow, or combinations. Two very popular and widely available varieties are 'Cheerfulness' and 'Golden Ducat'.

Triandrus hybrids. All are descended from the species *N. triandrus* and bear 1 to 6 flowers per stem. Subdivisions are based on whether the cup is more or less than two-thirds the petal length. They bloom in yellow, white, or white petals with yellow cups.

Cyclamineus hybrids. All are descendants of *N. cyclamineus*. They have one flower per stem, with petals curving back from the cup, which has wavy edges. Subdivisions are based on whether the cup is less or more than two-thirds the length of the petals. They come in yellow, yellow petals with red cup, or ivory petals with pink cup.

Jonquilla hybrids. Bred from the species *N. jonquilla*, these all have 2 to 6 flowers each. Subdivisions are based on whether the cup is more or less than two-thirds the length of petals. Available in yellow, ivory petals with pink cup, and yellow petals with red cup.

Tazetta and tazetta hybrids. All are descendants of the species *N. tazetta*. They have one cluster of 4 to 8 fragrant white flowers per stem, generally

Far left: *Narcissus* 'Pomona' (small-cupped daffodil)

Left: *Narcissus* 'Jonquilla Simplex' (jonquilla hybrid)

Below left: *Narcissus* 'Mary Copeland' (double narcissus)

with yellow or orangish cups. This group includes those popular for forcing, such as the Chinese sacred lily, 'Paper-white', and 'Soleil d'Or'.

Poeticus (or poet's) narcissus. Originally hybridized from *N. poeticus*, these usually have one fragrant white blossom per stem, with a shallow cup of contrasting color.

Species narcissus and wild hybrids. Small or miniature daffodils: *N. bulbocodium*, the petticoat daffodil, in bright yellow; *N. cyclamineus*, the cyclamen-flowered daffodil, in yellow; *N. jonquilla*, a sweetly fragrant yellow jonquil; *N. juncifolius*, the rush-leaved daffodil; *N. triandrus*, angels-tears, with clusters of small white flowers.

Miscellaneous. This category includes all narcissus that don't fall into one of the other categories, including those with split cups and hybrids of *N. bulbocodium*, the petticoat daffodil.

Cut *Narcissus* when the flowers are almost fully opened. They will stay fresh for a week.

Plant all *Narcissus* in full sun or partial shade as soon as they are available in early fall. Apply bone meal, as discussed on page 68. All *Narcissus* are winter-hardy in Zones 4 through 10, except for tazetta types (which are hardy south of Zone 8) and the petticoat, cyclamen-flowered, and rush-leaved daffodils (which are hardy in Zone 6 and south).

Narcissus are the best of the large-flowered bulbs for naturalizing. For directions on growing indoors or forcing of tender bulbs, see pages 55 and 57.

Narcissus 'Suzy' (tazetta hybrid)

Narcissus 'Thalia' (triandrus hybrid)

Narcissus bulbocodium

Nerine bowdenii

Nerine (Guernsey Lily)

These members of the Amaryllis family originated in South Africa. In late summer or fall, their unusual funnel-shaped, segmented flowers, which are borne in round clusters of 12- to 18-inch stalks, are exquisite in bouquets. The straplike foliage may appear along with or after the flower stalks, and some species remain green all year.

Flowers of *Nerine bowdenii* and its varieties are 3 inches long and borne in clusters of 8 to 12. Colors may be pale pink with dark pink lines, magenta, crimson, bright red, or silvery pink.

N. filifolia bears rose-pink blooms in clusters of 5 to 10 and has grassy, evergreen foliage.

N. undulata has clusters of 10 to 15 bright pink flowers and its foliage remains green most of the year.

N. curvifolia 'Fothergillii Major' is striking, with scarlet flowers brushed in shimmering gold and very long filaments topped by greenish anthers. *N. sarniensis*, or Guernsey lily, grows to a height of 24 inches with clusters of iridescent, deep red flowers.

Plant nerines in late summer or fall. They are hardy only in the warmest regions of the United States, and thus are usually container grown. Plant in the soil mix suggested on page 68 and do not water until flower stalks appear. Then keep the soil evenly moist and apply a balanced fertilizer monthly as long as the foliage is growing. Stop watering and feeding deciduous species in the summer. Keep evergreen plants barely moist through the summer. Store containers in bright light in a place above 60°F. during winter. Do not repot more often than every 4 to 5 years to increase blooming.

Ornithogalum (Chincherinchee, Pregnant Onion, Star-of-Bethlehem)

Ornithogalum will provide interest in the garden and a supply of long-lasting, beautiful blooms for cutting.

Two are commonly called star-of-Bethlehem. *Ornithogalum arabicum* produces clusters of 2-inch white flowers with a waxy texture. These are centered with shiny black pistils that inspired the other common name for the species, Arab's eye. Foliage consist of leaves to 24 inches that flop casually. The flower stalk also grows to 24 inches. *O. umbellatum* produces shorter stems, about 12 inches, with clusters of 1-inch white flowers that are striped with green on the outside. The blossoms close at night.

A very popular florist flower is *O. thyrsoides*, or chincherinchee. Star-shaped 2-inch white flowers with brownish-green centers are borne in tapering clusters on 2-foot stalks. Leaves stand upright and are about 2 inches wide and up to 12 inches long.

Ornithogalum arabicum

O. caudatum is a somewhat ungainly houseplant that is raised for its unique method of propagation. It is grown with most of the bulb above the soil line. Bulblets form under the tunic, swell, and finally split the tunic in a manner that suggests its common name: pregnant onion. (See the photograph on page 30.)

Ornithogalum flowers will keep fresh in an arrangement for more than a week. Pick them when the flower cluster is half open. The weak stems tend to droop. Either wind thin wire around them (see page 54) or bind several flowers together in a bunch.

Plant ornithogalums during the fall in bright sun. *O. umbellatum* is hardy as far north as Zone 4; the other two, only as far north as Zone 7. All make splendid container plants for indoors or out. In the garden no special care is required other than winter mulching in cooler areas.

Indoors, grow ornithogalums in the soil mixture suggested on page 68. Follow instructions there for growing plants in containers.

Oxalis (Good-Luck Leaf Plant, Lucky Clover, Wood Sorrel)

Many species of *Oxalis* are considered weeds in the garden, but a few are too pretty to be so labeled. Most grow in mounds of fine foliage from 4 inches to 12 inches across. Flowers about 1 inch in diameter cover the top.

O. adenophylla, the Chilean oxalis, produces a compact rosette of leaves topped with lavender-pink flowers that are richly veined. *O. bowiei*, or the Bowie oxalis, has leaves that resemble clover, and pink to purple flowers that may grow as large as 2 inches. Small, cloverlike foliage and rosy flowers are characteristic of *O. hirta*. The year-round bloomer of the genus is *O. crassipes*, producing pink or white flowers. Winter pink or white flowers grow on *O. purpurea* 'Grand Duchess'. Rosette oxalis, *O. deppei*, flowers in red or white during spring.

The Chilean oxalis is hardy outdoors to Zone 6. The others need warmer temperatures. If you plant them in the garden, plant the bulbs in late summer (August) in full sun or partial shade.

Cool-weather gardeners usually grow oxalis in pots placed where they can get 4 hours of sun per day and night temperatures above 60°F. Oxalis is very popular in greenhouses for winter bloom. Let the bulbs dry out gradually after flowering.

Polianthes (Tuberose)

The sweet fragrance of tuberoses is almost overwhelming. One or two cut blooms will perfume a room. This native of Mexico bears small tubular white flowers in a loose cluster on stems to 36 inches. The basal foliage is narrow and grassy. Select *Polianthes tuberosa* in either single or double form.

Far left: *Oxalis* species
Left: *Polianthes tuberosa*

All photos: *Ranunculus asiaticus* cultivars

Cut flowers when the spikes are half open. Many cultivars will need to be wired (see page 54) to keep them from drooping.

Plant tuberoses during spring after the temperature has risen above 60°F. at night, in full sun or partial shade. Feed monthly after the plants emerge from the soil, and then until the buds show color. *Polianthes* has a long growing season; cool-region gardeners should start the tubers in containers indoors about 6 weeks before temperatures can be expected to reach their requirements.

Dig up the thickened rhizomes after the tops brown. Dry and store them for the winter in a warm place. Since tuberoses do not always bloom the second year and the rhizomes are inexpensive, many gardeners treat the plant as an annual and buy new rhizomes each year.

To grow tuberoses in pots, plant about 3 rhizomes in a 6-inch pot. Store in a very warm place or use bottom heating coils until the plants root. Place the pots in direct sun after the plants are rooted. Water well during active growing.

Puschkinia (Striped Squill)

This extremely hardy bulb is native to the uneven terrain from Lebanon to Afghanistan. A dainty plant, *Puschkinia scilloides* grows only 6 inches tall. It is excellent in the rock garden or naturalized in drifts under trees or in front of shrubbery. It produces a rosette of strap-like leaves and bell-shaped flowers in loose racemes of 6 to 12 per stem. They are pale blue, opening flat, revealing a bluish-green stripe down the center of each petal. 'Alba' is a rare white form.

Puschkinia should have a well-drained gritty soil amply amended with leaf mold. It has a distinct preference for limey, alkaline soil. Plant the bulbs in fall, 3 inches deep and 3 inches apart. They are best used as generous drifts of at least 20 or 30 bulbs.

Ranunculus (Buttercup)

Flowers of *Ranunculus asiaticus* look as though they were made from rolled-up tissue paper in a host of pastels and bright colors. These gay additions to the landscape are commonly known as some sort of buttercup—Persian, French, Dutch, Scotch, turban, or double. Indeed, the common buttercup is a member of the same genus. The cheerful flowers measure from 2 to 5 inches in diameter on stems 18 to 24 inches tall. They continue to bloom for several months, so they are excellent for cut flowers. Just one plant may produce as many as 75 flowers during the season, which is late spring to summer, depending upon the climate.

Cut flowers stay fresh for more than a week. Cut them when they are almost fully open.

In Zones 8 through 10, plant during fall in full sun. In other zones, plant during spring. The tubers root better if they are soaked in water for several hours before planting. Plant them with the prongs facing downward. *Ranunculus* enjoy cool nights and sunny, but not hot days. Away from coastal regions they grow best in greenhouse culture. In all zones, dig up roots after the foliage withers, and store in a warm, dry place.

Scilla (Bluebells, Squill)

Not all bluebells are blue; some are purple, violet, pink, rose, or white. But all the following members of the genus *Scilla* produce bell-shaped blossoms borne in clusters on leafless stalks. Some produce as many as 100 blooms per stalk; others, no more than a few. Basal leaves of the plants are strap-shaped. Although bluebells are most attractive when sprinkled in a woodland garden, they are also attractive in pots.

Scilla bifolia is the earliest-blooming bluebell and is known as two-leafed squill. The blooms resemble open bells or stars in turquoise, white, violet,

Right: *Scilla peruviana*
Below: *Endymion hispanicus*

or purplish pink. Up to 8 flowers about 1 inch across are carried on stems that grow to 8 inches.

The Spanish bluebell, actually *Endymion hispanicus*, a close relative of the scillas (usually listed as *S. hispanica* or *S. campanulata*), is the most popular species. Its 15- to 20-inch stems carry about 12 nodding bells half an inch across. Varieties are available in white and pink, as well as in blue.

The English bluebell, *Endymion non-scriptus* (often listed as *S. non-scripta* or *S. nutans*), is also known as the wood hyacinth. Its bells are smaller than those of the Spanish bluebell, and the stalks grow only to 12 inches. It forms a carpet of blue in spring, or you may choose white or pink variations.

In spite of their name, Peruvian bluebells or squills are native to the

Mediterranean region. *S. peruviana* flowers are bluish-purple and borne in a dramatic, dome-shaped cluster instead of the gentle, elongated clusters of the other scillas. Stalks are 10 to 12 inches high. A single plant in a large pot makes a striking patio accent.

S. tubergeniana blooms in late winter or early spring. It produces only 1 to 4 flowers clustered along 5-inch stalks, but each bulb sends up several stalks.

Cold-weather gardeners take special delight in Siberian squill, or *S. siberica*, with dainty, flaring, intense-blue bells on 3- to 6-inch stems. This is one of the best for naturalizing—especially under deciduous trees.

Cut scillas for the house when half the spike has opened its flowers. They will last for up to a week.

Plant scillas in the fall in sun or partial shade. All species need plenty of moisture during the growing season. They also prefer being left alone for several years. See the chart on page 52 to determine which scillas are hardy to your zone.

Don't overlook scillas for an indoor garden. They make lovely houseplants. Follow directions on page 55.

Sinningia (Gloxinia)

Two species of *Sinningia* are grown as household accents or in the greenhouse. *S. speciosa*, or gloxinia, produces 3- to 6-inch bell-shaped blooms in shades of red through purple, as well as white. Its fuzzy foliage resembles that of another member of the Gesneriad family, the African violet, but the leaves are larger. Some gloxinias have double flowers; others are multicolored or edged with another color. Although this plant can bloom at any time of year, it requires a 2- to 3-month rest period between flowerings.

A miniature species, *S. pusilla*, is one of the tiniest of flowering plants. It produces exquisite lavender flowers that are only about ½-inch long on plants less than 3 inches across. Unlike the larger gloxinias, it does not have a noticeable period of dormancy.

Plant gloxinia tubers any time. They grow best in bright light, but not direct sun. Some people report success with 14 to 16 hours of fluorescent light each day. Night temperatures should stay above 65°F. Plant in the soil

Left: *Sinningia speciosa*
Below and bottom: *Sinningia* hybrids

Sinningia pusilla

mixture suggested on page 68. Water and fertilize each month from the time sprouts first emerge until the foliage begins to wither after blooming. Let the plant rest in a spot that is out of the way but still warm, until new growth begins in about 2 months. Repot it and begin the same culture.

S. pusilla should be kept evenly moist all year. Feed monthly with a liquid houseplant food. These plants bloom best if given 4 hours of direct sun a day. Miniature sinningias are often grown in tiny teacups, or even in thimbles that have holes drilled for drainage.

Sparaxis (Harlequin Flower, Sparaxis, Wandflower)

Harlequin flowers, *Sparaxis tricolor* and its hybrids, are among the most colorful members of the garden. Red, yellow, orange, purple, blue, mauve, and white flowers have patches of contrasting colors and triangular black spots at the base of each petal. The blooms are clustered along the end of a 12- to 18-inch spike. The foliage of this South African native is sword-shaped, like that of the gladiolus.

Sparaxis is hardy only in the warmest regions of the country and cannot tolerate much moisture. Plant in full sun during the fall.

In most of the United States, plant the corms in containers that can be protected during cold weather.

Sparaxis tricolor

Sprekelia (Aztec Lily, Jacobean Lily, St. James Lily)

From sunny Mexico comes the Aztec lily, *Sprekelia formosissima* (sometimes *Amaryllis formosissima*), also known as Jacobean lily or St. James lily. The flower is unusual: it looks more like an orchid than it does a lily. Flower stalks grow to 18 inches.

In warm areas, plant bulbs in the fall in full sun. In cooler regions, wait until frost danger is past in the spring. From Zone 7 north, dig up plants before the first frost and store them for the winter.

Sprekelia makes a striking houseplant and can be planted at any time. Follow directions on page 55 for care. Repot every few years.

Sternbergia (Fall Crocus)

Very similar in appearance to *Crocus*, *Sternbergia* differs chiefly in the number of stamens per flower. The bright yellow flowers of *Sternbergia lutea* appear in autumn, and usually precede the leaves. It is a native of the Caucasus and Asia Minor.

Sternbergia is not the easiest bulb to grow, requiring just the right conditions to thrive. This includes open, sun-baked soil that is very well drained, and is probably best grown only in areas of mild winters. It tolerates, even prefers, limey, alkaline soil. Plant the bulbs in June, 4 inches deep and 6

Sprekelia formosissima

Sternbergia lutea

inches apart. They should be left undisturbed, and in 6 to 8 years will form sizable clumps. Only after 2 to 3 years following planting will they start to bloom well.

Sternbergias are excellent for pot culture. Plant them in April or May, 4 to 5 bulbs to a pot, about 2 inches deep. Equal parts of loam, leaf mold, and limestone gravel is recommended. Place in a cool,dark place for about 6 weeks so that roots can form, then set outdoors in a sunny spot and water only sparingly. Increase water as buds appear. After flowering is complete, keep the plants growing through winter into late spring in a cool room, or outside in mild climates. Then, as the leaves die back, gradually withhold moisture. Do not repot these bulbs for several years; they bloom best when potbound.

Tigridia pavonia

Tigridia (Shell Flower, Tiger Flower)

Tiger flower or shell flower, *Tigridia pavonia*, blossoms in the summer with 5- to 6-inch flowers, each with 3 large flared segments and 3 very small inner ones. Colors include white, yellow, orange, scarlet, lilac, and buff. The bloom is borne on a 2-foot or taller stalk and is heavily spotted at its center. Flowers last only one day, but a succession of flowers provides for a long blooming period. Swordlike leaves grow to 18 inches, with smaller leaves growing on the tall flower stalk.

Plant *Tigridia* corms in spring when night temperatures reach 60°F., in full sun. Feed with a complete fertilizer twice a month and keep soil moist during active growth. Dig up and store after leaves turn yellow in Zones 7 north.

Tritonia (Flame Freesia, Montbretia)

A lookalike relative of *Gladiolus, Ixia, Sparaxis*, and *Freesia* is this South African native, sometimes known as *Montbretia*. Foliage is narrow and grassy. *Tritonia crocata* is sometimes dubbed the saffron tritonia, but is more frequently called flame freesia due to the appearance of its bloom. Unfortunately, however, it lacks the freesia's fragrance. Orange to red, funnel-shaped, 2-inch blossoms are loosely clustered along 12-inch branched, thin stems. *T. hyalina* also has brilliant orangey flowers, but the segments are narrower and transparent toward the base.

Tritonia hyalina

Tritonia is a tough, almost weedy plant in Zones 8 to 10, adapted to planting along roadsides and other areas that are not tended.

Plant the corms in the fall in full sun. In cool regions, wait until spring when temperatures at night reach 60°F. To get the most flowers, fertilize with a complete fertilizer every 2 weeks and keep moist during active growth. From Zone 7 north, dig up corms every year after the leaves yellow.

Tulipa (Tulip)

Modern tulip hybrids now number in the thousands, making them one of the most varied of the spring bulbs. Tulips are classified according to their time of bloom and their form. Except for the Rembrandt tulips and the species, all classes come in a wide range of colors.

Early flowering

Single early tulips. Large single flowers grow on 10- to 16-inch stems. Usually these are the first tulips to appear in the spring.

Double early tulips. Many-petaled, long-lasting double flowers, measuring up to 4 inches in diameter, grow on 6- to 12-inch sturdy stems.

Mid-season flowering

Mendel tulips. These are hybrids of crosses between Darwin and 'Duc van Tol', with single flowers on stems up to 20 inches.

Triumph tulips. Hybrids of single early tulips and late-flowering types. Stems are not over 20 inches.

Darwin hybrid tulips. Midseason flowers on stems up to 30 inches. Among the largest of all tulips.

Late flowering

Darwin tulips. Blooming late on stems 22 to 30 inches tall, these regal plants have large oval or egg-shaped blooms that are squarish at the base.

Lily-flowered tulips. These long, narrow blooms with pointed petals resemble lilies.

Cottage tulips. They are related to tulips found in old English and French gardens. Long oval or egg-shaped flowers; often have pointed segments.

Rembrandt tulips. These are late-flowering "broken" or mutated Darwin tulips. Striped or spotted on red, white, or yellow ground.

Below: *Tulipa* 'Dix's Favorite' (Darwin)
Below right: *Tulipa* 'Red Shine' (lily-flowered)

Parrot tulips. Late-flowering; 20 to 22 inches tall. Twisted, fringed, and ruffled blooms. May be striped, flamed, or marked with other colors, particularly green.

Double late tulips. Large blooms in orange, yellow, rose, or white grow on stems to 24 inches. Often called peony-flowered, due to their form.

Species tulips. Includes varieties and hybrids of the following: *T. fosterana*—early-flowering 4-inch blossoms on 8- to 20-inch stems. *T. greigii*—late-flowering, long-lasting blooms striped or matted on a scarlet or yellow ground, growing on stout 8- to 12-inch stems. *T. kaufmanniana*—the water-lily tulip, with pointed petals that open horizontally on 4- to 8-inch stems; early flowering.

Pick tulips when the buds are fully elongated, but before they open. The cut flower will stay fresh for up to a week. Cut tulips tend to turn toward the light. Give the vase a quarter turn every day to keep them facing in the direction you want. Tulip stems frequently are wired so that they can be easily curved in arrangements. See page 54 for instructions on wiring stems.

Tulips do not grow well in Zones 8 to 10 unless you purchase precooled bulbs or store them at 35° to 50°F. for 4 weeks before planting them in fall. In Zones 4 and 5, tulips need full sun or light shade. They will do better in partial shade in Zones 6 and 7. When shoots appear in spring, feed with a complete fertilizer. Precooled bulbs grown in warm climates should be discarded after blooming. Most tulips are hardy to Zone 3 if planted deeply enough. Tulips can be grown as houseplants. See page 55 for indoor planting details.

Tulipa 'Snowstar' (triumph)

Tulipa kaufmanniana

Tulipa 'Bellflower' (cottage)

Vallota (Scarborough Lily)

Native to South Africa, *Vallota speciosa* is quite similar to *Hippeastrum* and *Amaryllis*. From bright, glossy, evergreen leaves 2 feet long arise thick flower stalks to 2 feet high bearing 8 or 9 funnel-shaped flowers. Three inches across and vermillion red, the flowers are produced in August and September. Scarborough lily is almost exclusively grown in pots for indoor color.

Like most plants in the amaryllis family, it blooms best when potbound, so give it a pot that is 1 inch greater all around than the diameter of the bulb. Mix up some soil of equal parts loam, leaf mold, decayed cow manure, and coarse sand. In the bottom of the pot set down a layer of broken crockery. Then add a 1-inch layer of soil. Set in the bulb, and pack the soil around the bulb leaving the neck and shoulders exposed. The final soil level should be about 1 inch below the rim of the pot to allow for watering. Plant these bulbs in early summer.

At first, give them little moisture and grow them in as cool a room as possible. Increase water as foliage appears. The first year it is quite likely that only foliage will appear, with blooms appearing the second year. As *Vallota* is evergreen, never allow the bulb to dry out completely, but do reduce moisture each May and June, placing the pots outdoors in full sun. Increase the moisture at the end of June, and bring indoors into semi-shady conditions for flowering. Except for May and June, *Vallota* should be kept in semi-shade. Keep it moist during the autumn and winter.

Veltheimia

These South African natives are large bulbs with fleshy, wavy-edged leaves borne in basal rosettes. The flowers appear in late winter and early spring, drooping from a large conical truss. Veltheimias are best grown in a cool greenhouse, but can be successfully managed indoors in a sunny window.

Plant the bulbs in September, one bulb to each 5-inch pot. Provide gravel or broken crockery in the bottom of the pot for extra drainage, and use a light, friable soil that is high in organic matter. Set the bulbs in the soil so

Veltheimia species

Watsonia beatricis

that the top is left exposed. Water once thoroughly and place in a cool room for one month, allowing roots to form. Then set the pots in an even cooler, sunny room (45°F.—an unheated porch is great, as long as it remains above freezing) for the winter. Water sparingly. Do not splash water on the foliage. After flowering is complete, set the pots on their side in a sunny place to ripen the bulbs. Start them into growth again in the autumn.

Veltheimia capensis has pendulous flowers on a tubular truss that are pale pink with greenish tips. The flower stalks reach 16 inches.

Veltheimia viridifolia forms large inflorescences of 50 to 60 flowers at the end of 18-inch stalks. The flowers are a pinkish red, spotted with a pale yellow and shaded green at the edge.

Watsonia (Bugle Lily)

Reminiscent of the related *Gladiolus*, *Watsonia*, or bugle lily is a prolific summer bloomer. It bears 2½- to 3-inch tubular blossoms along flower spikes that tower above sword-shaped leaves. *Watsonia beatricis* is evergreen in warm climates, and 3½-foot stems bear apricot to red flowers.

In cool areas, plant *Watsonia* in the spring in full sun, or get a jump on the seasons and begin the corms indoors in pots about 2 months before the last frost is anticipated. Carry the pots to the garden, or transplant directly into the warmed earth. In the warm zones, plant in late summer to allow time for fall foliage production.

If you grow *Watsonia* in containers, follow instructions for indoor culture on page 55. Whether outdoors or in, the bugle lily should be kept evenly moist during the growing season and fed monthly with a balanced fertilizer. If you plant outdoors in cooler areas, dig up the corms after the foliage has been browned by the first frost. You'll probably need to stake the stems to keep them erect.

Zantedeschia (Calla Lily)

The regal calla lilies have been given a bad press: they have become so associated with funerals that they have almost gone out of favor. And in the West, many gardeners look upon them as pests. Yet no flower has a more perfect form; it is magnificent in the landscape and splendid as a cut flower.

The common calla lily, *Zantedeschia aethiopica*, produces a white to creamy 8-inch flower bract, or funnel-shaped spathe, surrounding an erect yellow spadix on a 3-foot, thick stem. The plant is a clump of 10-inch-wide and 18-inch-long leaves that grows to a height of about 4 feet. Baby calla, actually the cultivar 'Minor', is a smaller version; it has 4-inch flowers on 18-inch stems.

Zantedeschia aethiopica

But callas are not limited to the well-known white version. Golden yellow spathes are borne by *Z. elliottiana*, the golden calla. The flower is about 6 inches in length on an 18- to 24-inch stem. Its beautiful leaves are spotted in silvery white, and they measure about 6 inches wide and 10 inches long. The red or pink calla is *Z. rehmannii*, a smaller form than the other callas, which has 4-inch pink or rose-colored spathes. Its leaves are dotted with white. Look for hybrid calla lilies in purple, lavender, buff, and orange.

Pick flowers when they have fully opened. Buds and foliage are also popular for arrangements. But they are thirsty; watch the water level in shallow vases.

Plant callas outdoors in partial shade or in full sun as long as there is partial shade at midday. In Zones 8 through 10, callas can remain in the ground all year long. In other zones they will require spring planting and fall digging. After planting, water moderately until active growth begins; then give them plenty of moisture in well-drained soil.

All callas make stunning houseplants. Their culture is similar to that for other bulbs grown as houseplants (see page 55). Leave the plants undisturbed for several years, but each spring remove some of the old soil and add some fresh growing medium.

Zephyranthes candida

Zephyranthes (Fairy Lily, Flower-of-the-West-Wind, Raindrops, Rain Lily, Zephyr Lily)

Also known as rain lilies or raindrops because of their habit of appearing quickly after a rain, *Zephyranthes* are more universally called by such magical names as fairy lily, zephyr lily, or flower-of-the-west-wind. Their grassy foliage is evergreen on some species in warm climates, and these can flower intermittently all year, if the plants are kept alternately moist and dry.

Blooming in late spring or early summer in most areas is *Z. grandiflora*. This species bears 4-inch, rosy pink, funnel-shaped blossoms with 6 equal petals. The stems grow to 8 inches and the foliage is brownish near the base.

Midsummer brings the lemon-yellow, fragrant flowers of *Z. citrina*. In late summer or fall, *Z. candida* bears 2-inch flowers that are white on the inside and rosy pink on the outside.

Plant in full sun—during spring north of Zone 7, and during fall or late summer in the warmer regions. North of Zone 6 most gardeners dig up the bulbs in fall, but some report success with bulbs left in the ground when adequate mulching is provided. Normal garden culture is all these semi-hardy bulbs require.

Zephyranthes make attractive houseplants that can go outdoors when the weather warms up. Follow the guidelines on page 68, allowing the bulbs to rest for at least 10 weeks after the leaves wither.

Zigadenus species

Zigadenus

This native of North America and Siberia is closely related to *Camassia*. Loose racemes of greenish-white or yellow flowers are borne on 2-foot stalks that arise from tufts of slender, grass-like foliage. Open woodland conditions of rich soil high in organic matter and high filtered shade are strongly preferred. The flowers bloom in early summer, and the foliage remains attractive until autumn. As the leaves should not be cut back until they die down naturally, it is only useful in grassy meadows if the grass is left uncut all summer. Plant the bulbs in October, 3 inches deep and 9 inches apart, in groups of five or six. Leave them undisturbed for several years and allow them to multiply into sizable, dense clumps.

Zigadenus fremontii is the most attractive species with handsome grassy basal leaves and pale yellow starlike flowers, 1 inch across, in large racemes at the ends of 2-foot stems.

Zigadenus elegans bears short grassy leaves and small white flowers that eventually turn purple. It grows 18 inches tall.

Bunching onions

Edible Bulbs

Bulbous plants have been a part of the human diet since the beginning of civilization. People have eaten the bulb itself, the plant, the flowers it produces, or any combination of these. Bulbs that are merely decorative in some cultures are dietary staples in others. Few of us would consider making a salad of sliced tulip bulbs, chewing iris roots to freshen our breath, or baking bulbs of the butterfly orchid to accompany our roast beef. Yet what would our cookery be without bulbs such as onions, garlic, and scallions, or tubers such as potatoes?

Of course not all bulbs *are* edible. Several are poisonous to some degree: *Narcissus, Convallaria, Gloriosa, Colchicum, Zephyranthes,* and *Ranunculus*. American Indians and early settlers in this country ate many of the native bulbs and tubers, including *Camassia* (which is poisonous until it is cooked), *Calochortus, Brodiaea,* and several species of *Allium*.

The Egyptians grew *Iris* in their gardens to eat as an aphrodisiac. Later the Europeans used it as a breath deodorant. South American Indians preferred the bulbs of *Canna* as food over the flowers produced by the bulb. And in the Pacific Islands, the bulbous root of *Colocasia*, known as elephant's ears or taro, is still a staple food crop. For centuries, saffron harvested from the stigmas of the saffron crocus has been an expensive, distinctive seasoning much prized by gourmets.

This section takes a look at the bulbs and tuberous roots grown mainly as food.

Onion. This edible *Allium* species grows best in cool weather. It is so sensitive to day length that its varieties are classified as "short day" and "long day," so it is very important to select those that (according to catalogs or local garden centers) are best for your locality. The common onion is derived from *Allium cepa*, a native of western Asia.

Plant onions in well-fertilized soil, and supply continual moisture while the bulbs are forming. Begin onions from seeds, transplants, or sets (small dry onion bulbs). You can raise your own onion sets by broadcasting an ounce of seed over an area of about 4 square feet in fall (in Zones 8 to 10) or early spring (in colder regions). The seed will grow and make bulbs. However, due to the crowded conditions, the bulbs will be small.

Any variety of onion can be harvested when the bulb is small and the tops are lushly green. Most gardeners choose "bunching" perennial onions that do not produce large bulbs, but divide at the base to form new shoots throughout the growing season. The bunching onion is *Allium fistulosum* and is also from Asia.

Green onions, or scallions, are popular salad additions. Add chopped tops to soups, egg dishes, and entrees as garnish. Or cook whole green onions in water for 3 to 4 minutes, then drain, and serve with melted butter and a sprinkling of lemon juice—or top them with hollandaise sauce for an elegant addition to the meal.

When left in the ground to mature, onions produce bulbs that should be harvested and dried for future use. Onions will be sweeter if you cook them slowly. For an unusual main course, partially hollow out large onions and stuff them with any favorite meat, vegetable, or bread stuffing mix. Bake until tender.

Onion flowers, as well as the flowers of other *Allium* species, make beautiful garnishes on soups and other dishes.

Garlic. If you had to choose only one bulb to grow, you might just choose garlic. As beautiful as flowering bulbs are, what can compare to garlic, with its heady aroma and sweet yet pungent flavor? Choose from two types of garlic bulbs: small bulbs like those you find at the market, with about ten small cloves per head (*Allium sativum*); or 'Elephant Garlic', which grows up to six times larger and has a milder flavor (*Allium scorodoprasum*).

In cold regions, plant in the spring; elsewhere, in fall. Harvest the bulbs when the tops fall over. Store in a cool, dry place, or hang in bunches, or tie into braids.

Garlic is indispensable in Italian and French salad dressings. Simmered slowly in butter, it makes a great sauce for meats, fish, and vegetables.

Roman-style spaghetti sauce is made by slowly simmering minced garlic in good-quality green olive oil, then tossing with al dente pasta. Top with plenty of freshly ground Parmesan cheese.

For authentic Italian garlic bread, brush thick slices of French or Italian loaf bread with good olive oil and grill over charcoal or in the broiler. Rub freely with just-cut garlic cloves, drizzle with more oil, and sprinkle with salt and freshly ground pepper.

Chives. Chives (*Allium schoenoprasum*) and garlic chives (*Allium tuberosum*) are among the most attractive of the edible bulbs. If they are not cut for culinary purposes, they will produce a myriad of pink, cloverlike blossoms.

Grow chives from seed or buy small plants. They multiply rapidly, and a small bunch will soon become a large one. They make excellent borders in the vegetable garden or around a flower bed.

Chives are most easily harvested with a pair of scissors, and then snipped into salads, cottage cheese, or dips.

Garlic chives are a slightly larger relative and are especially good for imparting a slight garlic flavor to a salad. Garlic chives also make a beautiful potted ornamental.

Leeks can be harvested in winter.

Leek. The national symbol of Wales, leeks are said to grant a smooth and mellow singing voice to those who eat them regularly. Indeed, they are one of the mildest of the edible alliums.

Leeks (*Allium ampelloprasum*) are a slow-maturing, cool-weather vegetable. In the South, plant them during fall for a spring crop; in the North, set out transplants as early as possible. To blanch the stems, hill soil against them about 4 inches deep when the plants are a foot or so high. If you pull the largest leeks first, and break the flower stems off the remaining leeks as they form, you can extend the harvest for many weeks.

Leeks are attractive sliced into a salad. They also can be steamed or braised and served with a cream sauce. And of course they are an essential ingredient in that queen of summer soups, vichyssoise.

Chives are ornamental as well as edible.

Shallot. The shallot, famous for its use in French cuisine, is botanically a variety of *Allium cepa*. It is a "multiplier" type of onion, dividing into a clump of smaller bulbs that look very much like small tulip bulbs. Since most varieties set no seed, they are always grown from bulb divisions.

Although the bulbs are winter hardy in most places, you'll get better results if you dig and store the bulbs each year at the end of the growing season. Plant small new bulbs in the fall.

The flavor of shallots is somewhere between garlic and onions. They can be used in any of the ways you enjoy onions. When cooking shallots, chop them finely before sautéing. They should never be allowed to brown, but should be cooked until just tender.

Potato. The potato (*Solanum tuberosum*) is listed as the most important vegetable in the world and the fourth most important food plant. In the United States, more potatoes are eaten than any other vegetable.

The edible tuber is produced on underground stems from "seed" potatoes that are planted just before the last frost, when the soil is about 45°F. Fall crops should be planted 120 days before the first killing frost is anticipated.

Plant certified disease-free seed potatoes in a rich, loose, slightly acid soil with plenty of organic matter and a 5–10–10 fertilizer, as instructed on the package. Cut the potatoes into 1½-inch pieces, making sure that each piece has at least one good eye. Allow the cut surfaces to cure for about a week before planting. Gardeners often dip the pieces in diluted bleach or fungicide to prevent rot. You can skip this and plant small whole potatoes if you prefer. Plant the potatoes about 4 inches deep.

During the growing season, keep the soil evenly moist to a depth of at least 12 inches.

To pick new potatoes all summer, "plant" seed potatoes on the surface of prepared ground and cover with a foot or so of loose mulch, such as hay or sawdust. Potatoes will be formed between the mulch and the soil, beginning about the time you see the first potato flower. Harvest them weekly by exploring with your fingers under the mulch. Of course, you will not get any baking potatoes from this patch, because you are picking them before they have a chance to mature.

To store potatoes for the winter, allow them to mature before digging: wait until the vines yellow or die back. Dig and cure the potatoes in a dark place at 70°F. for about one week; then store between 35° and 40°F. in a place with high humidity.

When cooking potatoes, leave the skins on whenever possible for added nutrition, or peel thinly if you desire. Potatoes have been falsely accused of being fattening. In reality, however, they are relatively low in calories—a medium-sized baked potato has only about 75 calories—and are loaded with protein, minerals, and vitamin C.

To bake potatoes, wash the skins well, butter the skins, wrap in foil, and place them in a medium-high oven until tender, about 45 minutes. For a crisp skin, do not foil-wrap. Bake potatoes in a toaster oven if you like the skins extra crisp.

Sweet potato. A favorite edible tuberous root is the sweet potato. Native to Central and South America, it is actually a species of morning glory (*Ipomea batatas*). The plant needs hot weather in order to thrive.

Sweet potatoes are grown from slips produced by the parent tubers. You can grow your own slips or start with slips from mail-order seed companies or garden centers. Like so many other bulbous plants, sweet potatoes need well-drained soil.

Harvest when they are slightly immature, or as soon as the vines yellow. They'll taste best if they are stored first before they are eaten. Dry them in sunlight for 2 to 3 hours, move to a warm, humid storage area for about 2 weeks, then store at about 55°F. for 8 to 24 weeks.

Yams come from various species of *Dioscorea* and are darker and sweeter than sweet potatoes. Use less additional sweeteners when cooking them than you'd need with sweet potatoes. The simplest and best way to enjoy these tuberous roots is to bake them in their skins. Scrub the skins well and rub with butter. After cooking, split and add butter and a little honey or molasses if desired.

Try adding diced sweet potatoes to homemade chicken soup or vegetable soup for an unexpected sweet treat.

Mail-Order Bulb Suppliers

All the bulb varieties mentioned in this book can be bought from one or more of the suppliers listed here. Some of these suppliers specialize in bulbs. Others sell seed and nursery stock, but offer a selection of bulbs as well.

Many dealers offer two catalogs: a fall catalog that contains hardy bulbs for fall planting, and a spring catalog. The spring catalogs are the first heralds of the new year, appearing even before the crocus. They often contain seeds and nursery stock, as well as spring-planted bulbs such as begonias, cannas, and callas.

Many of these catalogs are the best sources of information about the culture of the bulbs they sell, so keep them for future reference. Many of them are beautiful as well, and all are interesting.

Breck's
6523 North Galena Rd.
Peoria, IL 61614
60 pages. Special emphasis on tulips, daffodils, and crocuses. Free.

Burpee Seed Co.
300 Park Ave.
Warminster, PA 18974
Besides its well-known seed catalog, Burpee also publishes 2 bulb catalogs, each about 50 pages. Free.

Cooley's Iris Gardens
Box 126
Silverton, OR 97381
60 pages. Specializes in tall bearded iris. The $2.00 cost is deducted from a minimum purchase of $7.50.

C. A. Crookshank
1015 Mt. Pleasant Rd.
Toronto, Ontario, M4P
2M1, Canada
General catalog. Issues an iris and poppy bulletin in June. The $1.00 cost is deducted from the first purchase.

De Jager Bulbs, Inc.
188 Asbury St.
So. Hamilton, MA 01982
30 pages. Offers a wide selection of common and unusual bulbs. Christmas minicatalog. Free.

Dutch Gardens, Inc.
Box 168
Montvale, NJ 07645
75 pages. Features Dutch bulbs and plants. Detailed descriptions and information. Makes a worthy addition to a catalog collection. Free.

Henry Field Seed and Nursery Co.
Shenandoah, IA 51602
General catalog. Free

Gurney Seed and Nursery Co.
1985 Page St.
Yankton, SD 57079
General catalog with a tabloid format. Free.

H. G. Hastings Co.
Box 4274
Atlanta, GA 31312
General catalog. Free.

International Growers Exchange
Box 397-X
Farmington, MI 48024
48-page Wide World of Bulbs and Plants *issued every 3 years. Straightforward itemizing. Two catalogs annually, plus bulletins describing rare and unusual bulbs. $5.00 puts you on the mailing list for 3 years; $3.00, for 1 year.*

Inter-State Nurseries, Inc.
Hamburg, IA 51640
General catalog. Free.

Jackson and Perkins
Box 1028
Medford, OR 97501
16-page fall catalog. Features a selection of tulips, daffodils, crocuses, and irises. Free.

J. W. Jung Seed Co.
Station 8
Randolph, WI 53956
General catalog. Free.

Kelly Brothers
23 Maple St.
Dansville, NY 14437
General catalog. Free.

Earl May Seed and Nursery Co.
Shenandoah, IA 51603
Fall bulb catalog. Offers tulips, daffodils, hyacinths, crocuses, and other bulbs. Free.

Messelaar Bulb Co., Inc.
150 County Rd.
Ipswich, MA 01938
19 pages of imported Dutch bulbs. Free.

Grant Mitsch Novelty Daffodils
Richard D. Havens
Box 218
Hubbard, OR 97032
28 pages. Special attention to novelty daffodils. Thoughtful, detailed descriptions. The $2.50 cost is deducted from the first purchase.

George W. Park Seed Co., Inc.
Greenwood, SC 29647
General catalog. Free.

Rex Lilies
Box 774-R
Port Townsend, WA 98368
72 pages listing hundreds of lily varieties. Cost is 10¢ in coin or stamps.

John Scheepers, Inc.
63 Wall St.
New York, NY 10005
65 pages. Carefully written and designed. Special attention to tulips, narcissus, dahlias, and lilies. Additional forcing edition around Christmas and supplements throughout the year. Free.

Schreiner's Iris Garden
3625 Quinaby Rd., NE
Salem, OR 97303
72 pages of irises. The $2.00 cost is deducted from the first order.

Van Bourgondien Bros.
Box A-245
Farmingdale Rd.
Babylon, NY 11702
51 pages of imported and domestic bulbs and plants. Offers rare and unusual bulbs. Free.

The Wayside Gardens Co.
Hodges, NC 29695
General nursery catalog packed with helpful information. The $1.00 cost is deducted from the first purchase.

White Flower Farm
Litchfield, CT 06759
General nursery catalog. Unique dictionary format with clear, interesting information. Black-and-white illustrations. Annual subscription of $5.00 includes two editions of The Garden Book *and three editions of* Notes. *The $5.00 cost is deducted from any order over $20.00.*

Plant Societies

Many bulb gardeners become fascinated with growing and observing a particular group of plants. If you find a bulb that intrigues you and want to learn more about it, consider joining a plant society. It will give you the opportunity to share experiences with other gardeners across the country who are especially interested in the same plants. In this way, bulb gardeners can benefit from one another's mistakes and triumphs. Membership in a plant society usually includes bulletins and other publications, as well as local and national meetings with gardeners who are intimately involved with the special plant that appeals to you.

American Begonia Society
1431 Coronado Terrace
Los Angeles, CA 90026
Membership ($4.00 annually) includes the monthly publication, The Begonian.

American Daffodil Society
89 Chicherster Rd.
New Canaan, CT 06840
Annual $5.00 dues include the Daffodil Journal, *published each quarter.*

American Dahlia Society
163 Grant Street
Dover, NJ 07801
Annual dues of $6.00 include the Annual Classification Book *and a quarterly bulletin.*

American Gesneriad Society
11983 Darlington Ave.
Los Angeles, CA 90049
Annual membership fee of $5.25 includes a bimonthly magazine.

American Gloxinia and Gesneriad Society
Box 174
New Milford, CT 06776
Annual dues ($6.00) include The Gloxinian, *published bimonthly.*

American Iris Society
2315 Tower Grove Ave.
St. Louis, MO 63110
Annual membership is $7.50. Members receive the AIS Bulletin *each quarter.*

American Plant Life Society and The American Amaryllis Society Group
Box 150
La Jolla, CA 92038
Membership is $5.00 annually, and includes both Plant Life *and* Amaryllis Yearbook.

American Rock Garden Society
99 Pierpoint Rd.
Waterbury, CT 06705
Annual dues of $5.00 include the society's quarterly bulletin.

Directory of Common Names

Common Name	Botanical Name
adder's tongue	*Erythornium*
African corn lily	*Ixia*
African lily	*Agapanthus*
amaryllis	*Hippeastrum*
amaryllis	*Lycoris*
Amaryllis	*Amaryllis*
Amazon lily	*Eucharis*
angel's tears	*Narcissus*
autumn crocus	*Colchicum*
Aztec lily	*Sprekelia*
basket flower	*Hymenocallis*
belladonna lily	*Amaryllis*
bluebeard lily	*Clintonia*
bluebells	*Scilla*
bugle lily	*Watsonia*
buttercup	*Ranunculus*
butterfly iris	*Moraea*
butterfly tulip	*Calochortus*
calla lily	*Zantedeschia*
camass	*Cammassia*
cat's ear	*Calochortus*
checkered lily	*Fritillaria*
chincherinchee	*Ornithogalum*
climbing lily	*Gloriosa*
crown imperial	*Fritillaria*
daffodil	*Narcissus*
desert-candle	*Eremurus*
dog-tooth violet	*Erythronium*
Easter bells	*Erythronium*
Easter lily	*Lilium*
fairy lily	*Zephyranthes*
fairy lantern	*Calochortus*
fall crocus	*Sternbergia*
fawn lily	*Erythronium*
firecracker flower	*Brodiaea*
flame freesia	*Tritonia*
flower-of-the-west-wind	*Zephyranthes*
fortnight lily	*Moraea*
foxtail lily	*Eremurus*
globe tulip	*Calochortus*
glory lily	*Gloriosa*
glory-of-the-snow	*Chionodoxa*
gloxinia	*Sinningia*
golden garlic	*Allium*
good-luck leaf plant	*Oxalis*
grape hyacinth	*Muscari*
grass-nut	*Brodiaea*
Guernsey lily	*Nerine*
guinea-hen tulip	*Fritillaria*
harlequin flower	*Sparaxis*
hurricane lily	*Lycoris*
hyacinth	*Hyacinthus*
Ithuriel's spear	*Brodiaea*
Jack-in-the pulpit	*Arisaema*
Jacobean lily	*Sprekelia*
jonquil	*Narcissus*

Common Name	Botanical Name
kaffir lily	*Clivia*
lily	*Lilium*
lily-of-the-Altai	*Ixiolirion*
lily-of-the-Amazon	*Eucharis*
lily-of-the-field	*Anemone*
lily-of-the-Nile	*Agapanthus*
lily-of-the-valley	*Convallaria*
lucky clover	*Oxalis*
Madonna lily	*Eucharis*
Madonna lily	*Lilium*
magic flower	*Anemone*
magic lily of Japan	*Lycoris*
Mariposa lily	*Calochortus*
meadow saffron	*Colchicum*
montbretia	*Tritonia*
mouse plant	*Arisarum*
naked lady	*Amaryllis*
naked lady	*Lycoris*
nut orchid	*Achimenes*
peacock iris	*Moraea*
Peruvian daffodil	*Hymenocallis*
Peruvian lily	*Alstroemeria*
pregnant onion	*Ornithogalum*
pretty-face	*Brodiaea*
raindrops	*Zephyranthes*
rain lily	*Zephyranthes*
resurrection lily	*Lycoris*
St. James' lily	*Sprekelia*
satin bells	*Calochortus*
Scarborough lily	*Vallota*
shell flower	*Tigridia*
Siberian lily	*Ixiolirion*
sky-blue lily	*Ixiolirion*
snake's-head	*Fritillaria*
snowdrops	*Galanthus*
snowflakes	*Leucojum*
Sparaxis	*Sparaxis*
spider lily	*Hymenocallis*
spider lily	*Lycoris*
spring meadow saffron	*Bulbocodium*
squill	*Scilla*
star-of-Bethlehem	*Ornithogalum*
stars of Persia	*Allium*
striped squill	*Puschkinia*
tiger flower	*Tigridia*
trout lily	*Erythronium*
tuberose	*Polianthes*
tulip	*Tulipa*
wandflower	*Sparaxis*
widow's-tears	*Achimenes*
wild hyacinth	*Brodiaea*
windflower	*Anemone*
winter aconite	*Eranthis*
wood sorrel	*Oxalis*
yellow spider	*Lycoris*
zephyr lily	*Zephyranthes*

Index

Italicized page numbers refer to illustrations. The chart on page 142 gives the most popular common names with corresponding botanical names for easy reference to the index.

A
Accent, *35*, 82
Achimenes, 84–85
  andersonii, *84*
  bloom season for, 46, 50
  in containers, 46, 56, 69
  designing with, 45, 82
  as example of rhizomes, 27
  in greenhouse, 56
  planting of, 68, 69
  propagation of, 73
Agapanthus, 85
  Africanus, 85
  bloom season for, 46, 50
  in containers, 46, 69
  designing with, 45
  as example of rhizomes, 27
  history of, 13
  orientalis, 85, *85*
  planting of, 68, 69
  propagation of, 73
  umbellatus, 85
Allium, *73*, 85–86, 138–139
  albopillosum, 86
  ampelloprasum, 139
  azurem, 86
  bloom season for, 46, 50
  caeruleum, 86
  cepa, 138, 139
  christophii, 86
  designing with, 32, 43, 44, 45, 82, 84
  as example of true bulbs, 25
  flavum, 86
  forcing of, 57
  giganteum, 50, *85*, 86
  karataviense, 44, 86
  moly, 82, 86
  neapolitanum, *85*, 86
  planting of, 68
  propagation of, 73
  sativum, 138
  schoenoprasum, 139
  scorodoprasum, 138
  triquetrum, 86
  tuberosum, 139
Alstroemeria, *29*, 86–87
  aurantiaca, 50, 86, *86*, 87
  bloom season for, 46, 50
  in containers, 56
  as example of tuberous roots, 27
  history of, 13
  ligtu, 86
  planting of, 68
  propagation of, 73
Amaryllis, *73*, 87 (*See also Hippeastrum*; *Lycoris*.)
  belladonna, 43, 50, 67, 87, *87*
  bloom season for, 46, 50
  designing with, 43
  as example of true bulbs, 25
  fertilizing of, 67
  formosissima, 122
  hallii, 122
  history of, 13
  planting of, 68
  propagation of, 73
  radiata, 122
Anemone, *73*, 87–88
  apeninna, 43, 44, 87, 88
  blanda, 40, 43, 44, 45, 87, 88
  bloom season for, 46, 50
  coronaria, 44, 87, *87*
  as cut flower, 54
  designing with, 34, 40, 43, 44, 45, 82
  as example of tubers, 26
  fulgens, 44
  palmata, 44
  planting of, 68
  propagation of, 73
Angel's fishing rod. *See Dierama.*
Annuals, designing with, 32, 34
Aphids, 29, 79
Arab's eye. *See Ornithogalum arabicum.*
Arisaema, 88–89
  designing with, 82
  propagation of, 73
  sikokianum, *88*, 89
  triphyllum, 88
Arisarum, 89
  proboscideum, 89, *89*
  propagation of, 73

B
Babiania, *63*
Begonia, 89–93
  bloom season for, 46, 50
  as cut flower, 54
  designing with, 36, *37*, 45, 82
  as example of tuberous roots, 27, *27*
  evansiana, 93
  grandis, 50, 68, 82, 93
  in greenhouse, 56
  improved varieties of, 29
  planting of, *66*, 68
  propagation of, 73
  × *tuberhybrida*, 50, 68, 82, *90*, *91*
Blooming seasons, 46, 49–52
  manipulation of, by forcing, 57–63
Botrytis, 78, 79
Brevoortia ida-maia, 94
Brodiaea, 94, 138
  bloom season for, 46, 50
  capitata, 94
  coronaria, 94
  designing with, 43, 44, 84
  elegans, 94
  as example of corms, 26
  forcing of, 57
  grandiflora, 94
  hyacintha, 94, *94*
  ida-maia, 94
  ixioides, 94
  laxa, 43, 44, 94
  lutea, 94
  planting of, 68
  propagation of, 73
  pulchella, 94
Brown, Lancelot, 10
Brunsvigia rosea, 87
Bulb cuttings, 71, *71*
Bulbils, 72, *72*
Bulblets, *72*, *72*
Bulbocodium, 94
  bloom season for, 46, 50
  designing with, 44, 84
  as example of corms, 26
  planting of, 68
  propagation of, 73
  vernum, 44, 84, 94, *94*
Butchart Gardens, *12–13*, 36

C
Caladium, 95
  bloom season for, 46, 50
  designing with, 45, 82
  as example of tubers, 26
  × *hortulanum*, 95, *95*
  planting of, 68
  propagation of, 73
Calla lily. (*See also Zantedeschia.*)
  designing with, 34
  improvement of, 29
Callicorea rosea, 87
Calochortus, 95–96, 138
  albus, 95
  amabilis, 95
  amoenus, 95
  bloom season for, 46, 50
  coeruleus, 95
  designing with, 82, 84
  planting of, 68
  propagation of, 73
  venustus, 95, *95*
Camassia, 96, 138
  bloom season for, 46, 50
  cusickii, 96
  designing with, 40, 43, 82
  as example of true bulbs, 25
  forcing of, 57
  leichtlinii, 96
  planting of, 68
  propagation of, 73
  quamash, 40, 96, *96*
Candytuft, *34*
Canna, 96, *96*, 138
  bloom season for, 46, 50
  in containers, 69
  designing with, 82
  as example of rhizomes, 27
  × *generalis*, 96
  planting of, 68, 69
  propagation of, 73
Cardiocrinum, 97, *97*
  cathayanum, 97
  giganteum, 97
  giganteum var. *yunnanense*, 97
  propagation of, 73
Carpeting, 82
Checker lily. *See Fritillaria lanceolata.*
Chionodoxa, 98
  bloom season for, 46, 50
  designing with, 40, 43, 44, 45, 82, 84
  as example of true bulbs, 25
  luciliae, 40, 98, *98*
  planting of, 68
  propagation of, 73
  sardensis, 98
Chives, 139, *139*
Climate zones, *48*, 48–49
Clintonia, 98
  borealis, 98, *99*
  propagation of, 74
  umbellata, 98
Clivia, *23*, 99–100
  bloom season for, 50
  in containers, 46, 56, 69
  designing with, 45
  as example of true bulbs, 25
  in greenhouse, 56
  miniata, 99, *99*
  planting of, 68, 69
  propagation of, 74
Colchicum, 100, 138
  autumnale, 100, *100*
  designing with, 43, 44, 82
  as example of corms, 26
  fertilizing of, 67
  luteum, 100
  planting of, 68
  propagation of, 74
Coldframe, use of, in forcing bulbs, 60, *61*
Colocasia, 138
Color, 32, *33*, 34, *34*, *35*, 38, *38–39*, 40, *40–41*, *42*
Container gardening, 45, *45*, 46, *55*, 55–56, 68–69, *69*
Convallaria, 100, 138
  bloom season for, 46, 50
  designing with, 82
  as example of rhizomes, 27, *27*
  majalis, 24, 100, *100*
  planting of, 68
  propagation of, 74
Cormels, 72, *72*
Corms
  definition of, 22
  examples of, 26
Cottage gardens, 34
Crinum, 100–101, *101*
  history of, 13
  × *powellii*, 100
  propagation of, 74
Crocosmia, 101, *101*
  propagation of, 74
Crocus, *74*, 102, *102*
  bloom season for, 46, 51
  designing with, 32, 43, 44, 45, 82, 84
  as example of corms, 26, *26*
  forcing of, 57, 59, 60, *62*
  planting of, 68
  propagation of, 74
Cut flowers, 48, *54*, 54–55
Cutworm, spotted, 79
Cyclamen, *74*, 102–103
  bloom season for, 46, 51
  cilicium, 103
  in containers, 46, 56
  coum, 103
  designing with, 43, 45, 82
  europaeum, 103
  as example of tubers, 26
  in greenhouse, 56
  hederifolium, *102*, 103
  neapolitanum, 103
  persicum, 46, 51, 56, 68, *102*
  planting of, 68
  propagation of, 74
  purpurascens, 82, 103

D
Daffodil, *31*. (*See also Narcissus.*)
  as cut flower, 54
  designing with, 32, *38*, 40, *40*, *42*
  as example of true bulb, *24*
  forcing of, 57, *58*, 59, *61*, *62*
  history of, 10
  planting of, 66
Dahlia, *74*, *103*, 103–104, *104*
  bloom season for, 46, 51
  designing with, 32, 82
  as example of tuberous roots, 24, 27, *27*
  in greenhouse, 56
  history of, 13
  planting of, 68
  propagation of, 72, 74
Daisy, *39*
Depth of planting, 68
Design, basics of, 32–35
  changing concepts of, 10, *11*, 12
  and cultural requirements, 82
  in public bulb displays, 36, *36–37*
  specialized, 42–45, 82, 84
Dichelotema ida-maia, 94
  pulchellum, 94
Dierama, 105, *105*
  propagation of, 74
  pulcherrimum, 105
Dietes bicolor, 123
Dioscorea, 140
Disease, 78–81
Dividing, 71, *71*, 72, *72*
Dog-tooth violet, 14. (*See also Erythronium.*)
Dormancy, 22. (*See also Forcing.*)
Drainage, 64, *65*, 66
  and container plants, 55
Dry-soil bulbs, 82

E
Edible bulbs, 138–140
Endymion
  hispanicus, 130
  non-scriptus, 130
Eranthis, 105
  bloom season for, 46, 51
  cilicica, 105
  designing with, 43, 44, 45, 82, 84
  as example of tubers, 26
  forcing of, 57
  hyemalis, 44, 105, *105*
  mulching of, *70*
  planting of, 68
  propagation of, 74
Eremurus, 105
  bloom season for, 46, 51
  bungei, 105
  designing with, 82
  elwesii, 105
  as example of tuberous roots, 27
  himilaicus, 105
  planting of, 68
  propagation of, 74
  robustus, 105, *105*
  stenophyllus, 105
Erythronium, 105–106
  albidum, 44, 105
  americanum, 14, 44, 105, *106*
  bloom season for, 51
  californicum, 105
  citrinum, 105
  designing with, 43, 44, 82
  as example of corms, 26
  grandiflorum, 105
  hendersonii, 105
  oreganum, 105
  planting of, 68
  propagation of, 74
  revolutum, 105
  tuolumnense, 105
Eucharis, 106
  amazonica, 106
  bloom season for, 51
  in containers, 46, 56, 68
  designing with, 45
  as example of true bulbs, 25
  grandiflora, 106, *106*
  in greenhouse, 56
  planting of, 68
  propagation of, 74

F
Fairy wand. *See Dierama.*
Fertilizing, 64, 66–67, *67*
Forcing, 46, *47*, 48, 57–63
  of container plants, 69
Formal gardens, 32, 34, *34*, *37*
Fragrance, 34, 82
Freesia, 106, *107*
  bloom season for, 46, 51
  in containers, 46, 56, 68
  designing with, 45, 82
  as example of corms, 26, *26*
  in greenhouse, 56
  history of, 13
  planting of, 68
  propagation of, 74
Fritillaria, 106–107
  bloom season for, 46, 51
  designing with, 34, 43, 82, 84
  as example of true bulbs, 25
  imperialis, 10, 68, 82, 106, 107, *107*
  lanceolata, 107
  meleagris, 43, 106–107, *107*
  planting of, 74
  propagation of, 74
  pudica, 107
  recurva, 107
Frost dates, 49, 53
Fungus, 78, 79

G
Galanthus, 109
  bloom season for, 46, 51
  designing with, 43, 82, 84
  elwesii, 109
  as example of true bulbs, 25
  forcing of, 57
  nivalis, *108*, 109
  planting of, 68
  propagation of, 74
Galtonia, 109
  candicans, *108*, 109
  propagation of, 74–75
Garlic, 138–139. (*See also Allium.*)
Garlic chives, 139
Gladiolus, 109–110, *110*
  blandus, 109
  bloom season for, 46, 51
  byzantinus, 109
  carneus, 109
  × *colvillei*, 109
  designing with, 32, 40, 45, 82
  as example of corms, 22, 26, *26*
  in greenhouse, 56
  history of, 13
  × *hortulanus*, 109
  improved varieties of, 29
  planting of, 68
  propagation of, 75
  tristis, 82, 109, *109*
Gloriosa, 110, 138
  bloom season for, 51
  in containers, 46, 56, 68
  as example of tubers, 26, *26*
  planting of, 68
  propagation of, 75
  rothschildiana, 110, *110*
Glory-of-the-snow, designing with, 32. (*See also Chionodoxa.*)
Gloxinia, in greenhouse, 56. (*See also Sinningia.*)
Golden Gate Park, 36, *37*
Gophers, 79
Greenhouse, 56, *56*
Growing seasons. *See* Blooming seasons.

H
Hampton Court Palace, *37*
Harvesting, 78
Hippeastrum, 110–111, *111*
  bloom season for, 46, 51
  calyptrata, 111
  in containers, 46, *55*, 56, 68, 69
  designing with, 45
  as example of true bulbs, 25
  in greenhouse, 56
  planting of, 68, 69
  propagation of, 71, 75
History of bulbs, 10–21
Houseplants. *See* Container gardening.
Hyacinth
  in containers, 55, *55*
  designing with, 32, 34, *37*, *38*, *40*, *45*

forcing of, 57, *58*, 59, 60, 62
history of, 10
Hyacinthus, 111–112
bloom season for, 46, 51
in containers, 46
designing with, 44, 45, 82
as example of true bulbs, 25
orientalis, 82, *111*, 111–112, *112*
orientalis var. *albulus*, 112
planting of, 68
propagation of, 71, 75
Hybrids, 15–16, 21, 28–29
Hymenocallis, 112
bloom season for, 46, 51
calathina, 112
designing with, 82
as example of true bulbs, 25
in greenhouse, 56
narcissiflora, 112, *112*
planting of, 68
propagation of, 75
Hypoxis, 112–113
designing with, 84
hirsuta, 112, 113, *113*
propagation of, 75

I
Industry, bulbs as, 17–19, *28*, 28–30, *29*
Informal gardens, 32, *33*, *34*
Ipomea batatas, 140
Iris, *75*, 114–118, 138
bakerana, 44, 115
bicolor, 123
bloom season for, 46, 51
cristata, 118
danfordiae, 44, 45, 84, 115
designing with, 34, *35*, 40, 43, 44, 45, 82, 84
as example of rhizomes, 24, 27, *27*
as example of true bulbs, 25
forcing of, 57, 60
gracilipes, 118
history of, 14, 19–21, *20*, *21*
histrioides, 44, 45, 115
improved varieties of, 29
japonica, 118
pavonia, 122
planting of, 68
propagation of, 75
reticulata, 40, 43, 44, 45, 51, *53*, 57, 60, 82, 84, 115, *115*
sibirica 'Sparkle', *115*
soil for, 66
tectorum, 118
Iris borer, 79
Ismena calathina, 112
Ixia, 119, *119*
bloom season for, 46, 51
in containers, 56, 68
as example of corms, 26
in greenhouse, 56
history of, 13
planting of, 68
propagation of, 75
Ixiolirion, 119
bloom season for, 46, 51
designing with, 82
as example of true bulbs, 25
montanum, 119
pallasii, 119
planting of, 68
propagation of, 75
tataricum, 119, *119*

JKL
Japanese beetles, 80
Kensington Gardens, *35*
Keukenhof public gardens, 36, *37*
Landscaping. *See* Design.
Leek, 139, *139*
L'Escluse, Charles, 10, 14, *15*, 19
Leucojum, 119
aestivum, 44, 46, 51, 119, *119*
autumnale, 51, 119
bloom season for, 46, 51
designing with, 43, 44, *44*, 84
as example of true bulbs, 25
planting of, 68
propagation of, 75
vernum, 44, *44*, 51, 119
Lilium, *75*, 119–121
auratum, 120
bloom season for, 46, 51
canadense, 14
candidum, 68, 120
in containers, 68, 69
designing with, 43, 45, 82, 84
as example of true bulbs, 25
in greenhouse, 56
longiflorum, 120
martagon, 120
philadelphicum, 14
planting of, 68, 69
propagation of, 71, 72, 75
regale, 120
speciosum, 120
superbum, 120
tigrinum, 43
Lily, *30*
designing with, 32, 34, *38*, 40
as example of true bulbs, 22, *25*
forcing of, 57
history of, 14
Longwood Gardens, 36, *37*
Lycoris, 122
africana, 51, 122
aurea, 122
bloom season for, 46, 51
designing with, 82
as example of true bulbs, 25
planting of, 68
propagation of, 75
radiata, 122
squamigera, 51, 82, 122, *122*

M
Miniature gardens, 44, *44*
Mites, 80
Moist-soil bulbs, 82
Moraea, 29, 122–123
bicolor, 123
bloom season for, 46, 52
in containers, 46, 56, 68
designing with, 44
as example of corms, 26
iridiodes, 123
neopavonia, 122
neopavonia villosa, 122
pavonia 'Magnifica', 44
planting of, 68
propagation of, 75
tricuspidata, 122
vegata, *122*, 123
Mosaic disease, 78, 80
Mulching, 70, *70*
of container plants, 55
of forced bulbs, 60, 61
Muscari, 123
armeniacum, 82, 123, *123*
bloom season for, 46, 52
botryoides, 123
comosum, 123
as cut flower, 54
designing with, 32, 40, 43, *43*, 44, 45, 82, 84
as example of true bulbs, 25
forcing of, 57, 60
moschatum, 123
planting of, 68
propagation of, 75
racemosum, 123
tubergenianum, 123

N
Narcissus, 123–125, 138
bloom season for, 46, 52
bulbocodium, 44, 125, *125*
in containers, 46
as cut flower, 54
cyclamineus, 125
designing with, 32, 34, *37*, 43, 44, 45, 82, 84
as example of true bulbs, 22, 25, *25*
forcing of, *58*, 60, 62, *62*
jonquilla, 125
juncifolius, 125
minimus, 44
nana, 44
new varieties of, 28
planting of, 68
propagation of, 71, 76
tazetta, 62
tazetta var. *orientalis*, 62
triandrus, 125
Narcissus fly larvae, 80
Naturalized landscapes, 42–43, *42–43*
Nematodes, 80
Nerine, 126
bloom season for, 46, 52
bowdenii, 126, *126*
in containers, 56
curvifolia, 126
designing with, 45
as example of true bulbs, 25
filifolia, 126
in greenhouse, 56
planting of, 68
propagation of, 76
sarniensis, 126
undulata, 126

O
Old Westbury Gardens, 36, *36*
Onion, 138, *138*. (*See also Allium*.)
as example of true bulbs, 22, *30*
Organic matter, as soil amendment, 66
Ornithogalum, *76*, 126–127
arabicum, *62*, 126, *126*
bloom season for, 46, 52
caudatum, *30*, 52, 127
in containers, 56
as cut flower, 54
designing with, 43, 45, 82, 84
as example of true bulbs, 25
forcing of, 57, *62*
nutans, 43, 52, 82
planting of, 68
propagation of, 76
thyrsoides, 126
umbellatum, 43, 52, 82, 84, 126, 127
Oxalis, 127, *127*
adenophylla, 44, 52, 84, 127
bloom season for, 46, 52
bowiei, 52, 127
brasiliensis, 52
in containers, 56
crassipes, 127
deppei, 127
designing with, 44, 45, 82
as example of true bulbs, 25
in greenhouse, 56
hirta, 127
planting of, 68
propagation of, 76
purpurea 'Grand Duchess', 127

P
Pansy, *35*
Peacock iris, 29. (*See also Moraea neopavonia*; *M. tricuspidata*.)
Perennials, designing with, 34, *34*, *35*
Peruvian lily, 29. (*See also Alstroemeria*.)
Pests, 78–81
Planting, 67–68
of container plants, 68–69, *69*
site for, 66, *66*
Planting Fields Arboretum, 36
Plant selection, 64
Polianthes, 127, 129
bloom season for, 46, 52
designing with, 45, 82
as example of tubers, 26
planting of, 68
propagation of, 76
tuberosa, 82, 127, *127*
Potato, 139–140
as example of tubers, 24, *26*
Propagation, methods of, 70–72, *71*, *72*
of specific plants, 73–77
Public bulb displays, 36, *36–37*
Puschkinia, 129
designing with, 82, 84
propagation of, 76
scilloides, 129

R
Ranunculus, 129, 138
asiaticus, *128*, 129
bloom season for, 46, 52
designing with, 34, *35*
as example of tubers, 24, 26, *26*
planting of, 68
propagation of, 76
Rhizomes, definition of, 24
dividing, 71, *71*
examples of, 27
Rhododendron, *35*
Rock gardens, 44, 84

S
Saffron, 138
Scab, 78, 80
Scaling, 71, *71*
Scallions, 138
Scilla, *76*, 129–131
bifolia, 44, 52, 129–130
bloom season for, 46, 52
campanulata, 130
designing with, 40, 43, 44, 82, 84
as example of true bulbs, 25
forcing of, 57
hispanica, 130
non-scripta, 130
nutans, 130
peruviana, 52, 68, *130*, 131
planting of, 68
propagation of, 71, 76
siberica, 40, 44, 52
tubergeniana, 44, 52, 57, 131
Scoring, 71, *71*
Seeding, 71, *71*
Shade, 66, *66*, 82
Shallot, 139
Shell flower. *See Tigridia*.
Siberian lily. *See Ixiolirion*.
Sinningia, *131*, 131–132
bloom season for, 52
in containers, 46, 56
designing with, 45
as example of tubers, 26
planting of, 68
propagation of, 76
pusilla, 131, 132, *132*
speciosa, *76*, 131, *131*
Slugs, 81
Snails, 81
Soil, for forced bulbs, 59, 62
preparation of, *65*, 66
Solanum tuberosum, 139–140
Spacing, 68
Sparaxis, 132
bloom season for, 52
in containers, 46
designing with, 44
as example of corms, 26
forcing of, *63*
in greenhouse, 56
history of, 13
planting of, 68
propagation of, 77
tricolor, 44, 132, *132*
Speckled bead-lily. *See Clintonia umbellata*.
Spire lily. *See Galtonia candicans*.
Sprekelia, 132
bloom season for, 52
in containers, 46, 56
as example of true bulbs, 25
formosissima, 132, *132*
planting of, 68
propagation of, 77
Springfields public gardens, 36
Star grass. *See Hypoxis*.
Stem cuttings, 72, *72*
Sternbergia, 132–133
designing with, 82, 84
lutea, 132, *132*
propagation of, 77
Storing, 78, *78*
Summer hyacinth. *See Galtonia*.
Sweet potato, 140
as example of tuberous roots, *27*
Sycamore, *40*

T
Thrips, 81
Thunberg, Carl, 13
Tigridia, 133
bloom season for, 46, 52
as example of corms, 26
in greenhouse, 56
history of, 13
pavonia, 133, *133*
planting of, 68
propagation of, 77
Trillium, 82
Tritelleia, *hyacinthina*, 94
ixiodes, 94
Tritonia, 133–134
bloom season for, 46, 52
crocata, 133
as example of corms, 26
in greenhouse, 56
hyalina, 133, *133*
planting of, 68
propagation of, 77
True bulbs, definition of, 22
examples of, *24*, 25, *25*, *30*
Tuberose, history of, 13. (*See also Polianthes*.)
Tuberous roots, definition of, 24
dividing, 72, *72*
examples of, 27
Tubers, definition of, 24
examples of, 26
Tulip, *12–13*
as cut flower, 54
designing with, 32, 34, *34*, *35*, *36*, *37*, *38*, *39*, 40, *40*, *45*
as example of true bulbs, 22, *25*
forcing of, 57, 59, 60, 62
history of, 10, *11*, 14–19, *16–17*, *18*
new varieties of, 28
Tulipa, 77, 134–135
bloom season for, 46, 52
clusiana, 43
in containers, 69
designing with, 43, 45, 82, 84
as examples of true bulbs, 25
fosterana, 135
greigii, 135
kaufmanniana, 43, 135, *135*
planting of, 68, 69
propagation of, 70, 77
sylvestris, 82
tarda, 43

V
Vallota, 135
propagation of, 77
Varieties, creation/improvement of, 28–30
Veltheimia, 135–136, *136*
capensis, 136
propagation of, 77
viridifolia, 136
Verdier, 21
Victor, 21
Viola, *38*, *40*

WXYZ
Wandflower. *See Sparaxis*.
Watering, 64, 70
of forced bulbs, 59, 62
Watsonia, 136
beatricis, 136, *136*
bloom season for, 46, 52
as example of corms, 26
history of, 13
planting of, 68
propagation of, 77
Wildflowers, designing with, 32, 34
Wireworms, 81
Wood hyacinth. *See Endymion non-scriptus*.
World Flower Show, 36
Yam, 140
Yellow moraea. *See Dietes bicolor*.
Yellows disease, 78, 80
Zantedeschia, 29, 136–137
aethiopica, 56, *77*, 136, *136*
bloom season for, 52
in containers, 46, 56, 69
designing with, 44, 45
elliottiana, *83*, 137
as example of rhizomes, 27
in greenhouse, 56
planting of, 68, 69
propagation of, 77
rehmanii, 56, 137
Zephyranthes, 137, 138
bloom season for, 46, 52
candida, 56, 137, *137*
citrina, 56, 137
in containers, 56
as example of true bulbs, 25
grandiflora, 56, 137
planting of, 68
propagation of, 77
Zigadenus, 137, *137*
elegans, 137
fremontii, 137
propagation of, 77